CW00504370

COAY4L £2.99

GOETHE'S WEIMAR

Part Two of

EUROPA

a tetralogy

Poetry

Collected Poems 1960–1984
Nightingales: Poems 1985–1996

Plays

Agora — a Dramatic Epic,
in chronological order of action
consisting of:

Healing Nature — The Athens of Pericles
Virgil and Caesar ⎫
Moving Reflections ⎬ The Roman Trilogy
Light Shadows ⎭
Byzantium
Living Creation
A Conception of Love
Maquettes for the Requiem   Trilogy of one-act plays
Lying Figures ⎫
Killing Time ⎬ The Requiem Trilogy
Meeting Ends ⎭

Europa — a Brief Epic,
a tetralogy, the first two plays
of which are:

King Francis I
Goethe's Weimar

Editor

Eleven Poems by Edmund Blunden
Garland
Studies in the Arts

GOETHE'S WEIMAR

a play by Francis Warner

*Who can return sufficient thanks to a great poet, the most
precious jewel of a nation?*

Beethoven (of Goethe) to
Bettina Brentano.
Vienna, February 10, 1811

OXFORD THEATRE TEXTS 13
COLIN SMYTHE, GERRARDS CROSS, 1997

First published in 1997 by Colin Smythe Limited
Gerrards Cross, Buckinghamshire

Warner, Francis. 1937–
Goethe's Weimar : a play — (Oxford Theatre Texts,
ISSN 0141–1152; 13)

ISBN 0–86140–406–8

Distributed in the United States of America by
Dufour Editions, PO Box 7, Chester Springs, PA 19425

The author acknowledges his debt to *Titian : Nymph and
Shepherd* by John Berger and Katya Berger Andreadakis,
Prestel-Verlag (Pegasus Library), Munich and New York, 1996

Cover design and production photographs by
Billett Potter of Oxford

Produced in Great Britain
Printed and bound by
T. J. International Ltd., Padstow, Cornwall

FOR TIM PRENTKI

GOETHE'S WEIMAR was produced by the Oxford University Dramatic Society (OUDS) for performance in Christ Church Cathedral, Oxford on Tuesday, February 25th, 1997. The director was Tim Prentki.

The cast was as follows:

Goethe	*Daniel Cassiel*
Schiller	*Ian Drysdale*
Wieland	*Napoleon Ryan*
Herder	*Desmond Brady*
Hölderlin	*William Greener*
Kleist	*James Chapman*
Müller	*Ben Wright*
Gontard	*Ben Smith*
Napoleon	*Ian Drysdale*
Talleyrand	*Philip Meyer*
Metternich	*Desmond Brady*
Lord von Haza	*James Webb*
Boy, von Haza's son	*Benedict Warner*
Vogel	*Paulius Kunčinas*
Daru	*Matthew Hodges*
Prussian Officer	*Ben Smith*
First Tirailleur	*Matthew Widick*
Second Tirailleur	*Robert Stannard*
First Male Nurse	*Jeffrey Johnson*
Second Male Nurse	*Philip Meyer*
Duchess Anna Amalia	*Flavia Kenyon*
Charlotte von Stein	*Alice Hart Dyke*
Lotte von Schiller	*Emily Dickos*
Christiana Goethe	*Kathy Tozer*
Wilhelmine von Zenge	*Manfreda Cavazza*
Luise von Zenge	*Elizabeth Judge*

Amalie Wieland	*Michelle Richardson*
Karoline Wieland	*Sarah Byrd*
Luise Wieland	*Miranda Warner*
Susette Gontard	*Josephine Higgs*
Henriette Vogel	*Gayle Ashley*
Thusnelda	*Chaon Cross*
Soprano Soloist	*Alison Kane*

Lighting and Sound David Colmer with Jolene Rice, Katie Albright. Costumes Penelope Warner with the Royal Shakespeare Company, Royal National Theatre, Birmingham Costume Hire, and Leslie Hager. Hair styles Fiona Button. Slide projection and sound equipment from Lighting & Sound Equipment, Oxford. Accompanists Christ Church organ scholars Philip Millward, Clive Driskill-Smith, David Goode. Stewards Lara Buchan, Jessica Buck, Monica Casillas, Matthew Davies, Lindsay Dolce, Adrienne Frazier, Sarah Gerwig, Paul Goldner, Amy Johnson, Lindsay Johnson, Dana Quarles, Bryce Quillin, David Smith. Stage Manager Manfreda Cavazza. Associate Director Kathy Tozer. OUDS President Alex Potts.

Characters

Goethe
Schiller
Wieland
Herder
Hölderlin
Kleist
Müller
Gontard
Napoleon
Talleyrand
Metternich
Lord von Haza
Boy, von Haza's son
Vogel
Daru
Prussian Officer
First Tirailleur
Second Tirailleur
First Male Nurse
Second Male Nurse

Duchess Anna Amalia
Charlotte von Stein
Lotte von Schiller
Emilie Schiller, the Schillers'
    daughter
Christiana Goethe
Wilhelmine von Zenge
Luise von Zenge
Amalie Wieland
Karoline Wieland
Luise Wieland
Susette Gontard
Henriette Vogel
Thusnelda
Soprano Soloist

The play is set in Germany between the years
1794 and 1812 A.D.

There are two acts.

Act One

The Lutheran Town Church of St. Peter and St.
Paul, Weimar. Spring, 1794.
Memorial service for LENZ. *Procession enters.*
Mozart's 'Alleluia' (Motet: 'Exsultate jubilate'
K165). In the procession a bier is carried; on it lies a
large cross, wearing LENZ *'s coat and hat. Candles.*

HERDER   We gather here today to lay to rest
Our memory of one known to us all
In Weimar's church of Peter and Saint Paul:
The poet Jakob Michael Reinhold Lenz,
(Cross is raised up to display LENZ *'s coat and hat)*
Disciple of our Goethe, but expelled
For asinine behaviour from our town:
Found on a Moscow street, his life wrung dry.
(Cross is lowered flat on the bier again)
The music you have heard was by our loved,
So recent-lost, young Wolfgang Mozart, whose
Magic Flute plays at our theatre now
(Frau Weyrauch singing as the Queen of
      Night).
*(*HERDER *holds up tickets, implying they are for sale)*
To close, we ask our Privy Councillor,
As friend and hero of the playwright Lenz,
Wolfgang von Goethe – whose great ancestor
Lukas Cranach stares from his altar-piece,
With Luther pointing to the Holy Book,
As Christ is crucified on Calvary –
(Points to triptych above the altar)
We ask Herr Goethe to read from that Book
A warning wrenched from Lenz's wretched life,
Drawn from the *Book of Proverbs.*

GOETHE   *(Reading from Bible)*The lips of a strange woman
      drop as an honeycomb, and her mouth is

smoother than oil.

Stolen waters are sweet, and bread eaten in
    secret is pleasant:

But let thy fountain be blessed: and rejoice
    with the wife of thy youth.

Let her be as the loving hind and pleasant roe:
    let her breasts satisfy thee at all times; and
    be thou ravished with her love.

And why wilt thou, my son, be ravished with a
    strange woman, and embrace the bosom
    of a stranger?

For at the window of my house I looked
    through my casement,

And beheld among the simple ones a young
    man void of understanding,

Passing through the street near her corner;
    and he went the way to her house,

In the twilight, in the evening, in the black and
    dark night:

So she caught him, and kissed him, and with
    an impudent face said unto him:

This day have I paid my vows, therefore came I
    forth to meet thee,

Diligently to seek thy face, and I have found
    thee.

I have decked my bed with coverings of tapestry,
    with carved works, with fine linen of Egypt.

I have perfumed my bed with myrrh, aloes and
    cinnamon.

Come, let us take our fill of love until the
    morning: let us solace ourselves with loves,

For the goodman is not at home, he is gone a
    long journey:

He hath taken a bag of money with him, and
    will come home at the new moon.

He goeth after her straightway, as an ox goeth
    to the slaughter.

Can a man take fire in his bosom, and his
    clothes not be burned?

So is he that goeth in to his neighbour's wife;

he destroyeth his own soul;
For jealousy is the rage of a man: therefore he
    will not spare in the day of vengeance.

Exit Procession, singing.

SCHILLER   There goes Goethe, like Napoleon,
Godlike, unbeatable; an egoist,
With far more genius than I, and yet
He blocks my sunlight – that's why I detest him!
Though I adore his mind, appreciate
His greatness. One can't reach through his
    façade –
To me a haughty prude who must be raped
Till I have made him pregnant, and he lies
Brought down, humiliated, stripped, exposed
In front of all his adulating world.
He's had life easy: I still sweat for bread.
He glides with full-sailed dignity, while I,
Haggard, scruffy, chain-smoking, long-necked,
    walk
Like an old camel; tense, furrowed with
    coughing,
Peering around; a pain in my left lung ...
I'm always the last person people notice.
Imperial calm!
He charms all till they worship, but without
Giving himself; remote Olympian!
Why, I could kill his spirit – and then weep
Like Brutus, love this Caesar from my heart.
His calculated courtesies cry out!
I hate him – and admire. Why won't he take
Notice of me? I've lived here seven years,
Waiting to be his friend. He's forty-five.
I know I'm ten years younger, wake at noon,
Work through the night with coffee, unlike him!
Why won't that shot by which young Werther
    dies
In his great novel kill the author, too?
And, self-inflicted, redeem me from guilt?

SCENE TWO

Enter HÖLDERLIN.

HÖLDERLIN   Herr Doctor von Schiller?

SCHILLER   What the hell do you
          want?
          I'm praying. Who are you?

HÖLDERLIN   My name is Friedrich
          Hölderlin.

SCHILLER   I've never heard of you.

HÖLDERLIN   Well, as I'm only twenty-four this month,
          I'm not surprised; but I belong to you –
          Although I'm not a thing of much importance.
          I'm new to Weimar; missed this. Who are they?

SCHILLER   There's Herder, our spell-binding preacher.
                    He'd
          Published great work before he was your age!
          Doubtless his bones will underprop this church
          That J.S. Bach so loved he had his sons
          Ducked in that sandstone font. Duchess
                    Amalia!
          She dragged old Christoph Wieland – there he
                    goes! –
          To Weimar to be tutor to her son
          Karl August, now our Duke. The Duke brought
                    Goethe
          (Still the Duke's closest friend). Goethe invited
          Herder – his own great, harshest teacher – here
          To be the Duke's Court Preacher, and our
                    Pastor.
          Now you have seen the literary gods
          Who make small Weimar glow before the

world,
Parnassus on the Ilm, the German Athens ...
What do you mean, 'you're mine'?

HÖLDERLIN   That's why
              I've come.
Frightened by what is happening in France,
Yet drunk with news of Robespierre's
              guillotine,
I visited the inn in which you stayed
The night you fled Duke Eugen. That to me
Is holy. I had tears, wet on my cheeks,
Of admiration for you, and your play
The Robbers, as I stood where you had slept:
Your tense, impassioned, freedom-fury'd
              brigands
Seething within your tyrant-fleeing brain,
Great and inspired poet!

SCHILLER   Do you mock?
Here; I'm not used to this. When I was fresh
In Weimar, I was courteously received
By Herder, who knew nothing I had written.

HÖLDERLIN   Surely he'd heard talk of *The Robbers*?

SCHILLER   No.
(What are you holding?) Pancaked my self-
              respect.

HÖLDERLIN   Friedrich Stäudlin, editor of the *Chronik* –
That anti-Roman Catholic newspaper ...

SCHILLER   He edits more than that! His claim to be
The Pope of Swabian literature stung me
To wrest the sceptre from his flaccid grasp
With my own poems in a rival bid ...
That's long ago.

HÖLDERLIN   I'm sorry that I spoke.

SCHILLER   Why?

HÖLDERLIN   I think I'll leave.

SCHILLER   Not like that! Why?

HÖLDERLIN   Because this letter from Stäudlin to you
Recommends, for your friendship's sake,
      myself.

SCHILLER   *(Reads the letter)* You are a poet – yes; I should
      have guessed:
Need my support, encouragement!
      Employment?
Charlotte von Kalb at Waltershausen Castle
Needs a house-tutor. I shall write.

HÖLDERLIN   Thank you;
And will you read my poems?

SCHILLER   If I must:
I hope they're not all love. Live in Kalb's
      house,
Remote. The Major seldom visits wife
And child, garrisoned as he is at Landau,
(The boy you'll teach is nine). And write some
      more.
I'll knock your poems on great Goethe's door!
(Exeunt)

SCENE THREE

GOETHE *'s garden house.* CHRISTIANA *sola. Enter*
LOTTE SCHILLER.

LOTTE   May I come in?

CHRISTIANA   Frau Schiller!

LOTTE   Call me Lotte:
                    Agreed?

CHRISTIANA   Yes, Frau Schiller.

LOTTE   Are you alone?

CHRISTIANA   Herr Goethe is not here.

LOTTE   I'll visit you!

          CHRISTIANA *reaches for a bottle of wine and two
          glasses;* LOTTE *goes to the window.*

          This garden house of his looks right across
          The park, whose endless changing shades of
                green
          Set off by purple wild-flowers carpeting,
          Lift our eyes over picnickers to where
          The rippling, supple, racing, bending stream,
          Our river Ilm, lapping great tree-trunks' roots
          All silver-smooth, catches the flickering light
          As hidden stones gently delay the sound
          Before the swirling water speeds again
          Off under rustling, wing-brushed leaves that
                dapple
          Deflected bees along their honeyed way.

CHRISTIANA   I can see why Herr Schiller married you!

LOTTE   Our stream of life had boulders. When we met
                I was just twenty-one; my married sister,
                Caroline, was there too. I sighed; was shy –
                Caroline being more articulate,
                Sparkling, vivacious – well, just more mature.
                We both had read his works, and she could talk
                Fluently and intelligently. Worse –
                Charlotte von Kalb, married, had spidered
                      him.

CHRISTIANA   Entangled him?

LOTTE   She recommended him,
              Through her connections, and her husband
                  Heinrich's,
              To read Act One of his *Don Carlos* to
              The Hessian court at Darmstadt; groomed his
                  voice
              To read it well. She dressed him in new clothes.
              The chief guest in the audience was our
              Weimar Duke, Karl August, who gave him
              There, on the spot, a title to match hers:
              Well – 'Counsellor of Saxe-Weimar'.

CHRISTIANA   That
              Was kind of her!

LOTTE   Do you know his play?
              Don Carlos loves the Queen Elizabeth,
              His stepmother – forbidden passion! Rich
              Charlotte encouraged him to taste that fruit.
              When Schiller came to Weimar it was she
              Introduced him unashamedly
              As hers, at Goethe's birthday party. Bar
              Her son, she was his only friend in Weimar.
              She felt her fortune would bind him her man.

CHRISTIANA   What happened when you touched?

LOTTE   He thought
                  they'd parted.
              She didn't. She went for me, with her nails,
              Black and on fire – just like a Christmas pudding.
              And so, you see, I know what you are feeling –
              My Frau von Kalb, your Frau von Stein ... she's
                  here!

              Enter CHARLOTTE VON STEIN.

CHARLOTTE   Can it be true? Where is she? Ah! I see:

The flower-girl; uneducated. Fritz,
My little son, was right. Do you stay here?
I won't say 'live'. How old are you?

CHRISTIANA   Come in.
I'm twenty-three.

CHARLOTTE   Goethe could be your father!

CHRISTIANA   The Privy-Councillor is thirty-nine.

CHARLOTTE   Goethe, my former friend of fourteen years,
Has thrown away ten million vows of love
And a relationship so pure it will
Glow in the memory of Europe to
Turn his Italian heart away from me
(That country ruined him), our angel love,
To slum his genius on a common whore.
I'll see his mother ...

LOTTE   Gently, Charlotte; come,
You are annihilating her.

CHARLOTTE   Ha! She'll go
Back to old Bertuch's flower factory.
How did they meet?

LOTTE   Shall we ask Christiana?

CHRISTIANA   Please may I say? Although I'm here alone,
And you great ladies are beyond my world,
If we must talk, would you like to sit down?
(LOTTE *and* FRAU VON STEIN *sit.* CHRISTIANA
remains standing)
Goethe was walking in this park outside,
And I approached him, as he'd been to see
All of us in the attic sewing-room
In Bertuch's house, cutting out taffeta
And silk to make court-flowers for your dresses.

CHARLOTTE   What insolence!

LOTTE   But tell us what you said.

CHRISTIANA   My parents have both died. My brother August
Is a hard worker, and supported all
Us children – and through no fault of his own
Has lost his job. We've nothing. Madam: no.
I'm not a whore.
That's why I had the courage to approach
The Privy Councillor.

CHARLOTTE   He brought you here,
To this pure shrine he sanctified to me –
Goethe, our intellectual Prince of Weimar;
My Wolfgang, genius, Germany's high star –
And skirt-lifted, bedded you!

CHRISTIANA   *(Stung)* That is
        not true!
Herr Knebel was still living here! You may
Be mighty ladies, and as such I bow,
But he is kind to me, and writes me poems.

CHARLOTTE   You grotesque! Writes *you* poems?

LOTTE   Hold your
        breath.
To strike a servant girl is social death.
Christiana, this is not the time
To chat with you over a glass of wine ...

CHARLOTTE   He was not man enough to tell me this –
Austere, devoted, virtuous – a coward ...

CHRISTIANA   Madam; I think you have a loving husband;
Chief Equerry, companion of our Duke?
And you are forty-six; twice my age?

CHARLOTTE   Slut!
You strumpet shaped just like a coconut!

Our love so cherished, and my supreme friend
In whom I joyed, destroyed, and at an end.

Fade.

SCENE FOUR

GOETHE *and* SCHILLER *walking home. July.*

GOETHE   What did you think of August Johann Batsch's
Lecture?

SCHILLER   Do you know him? He's a friend?

GOETHE   I met him ice-skating, and liked him.

SCHILLER   Doubtless
You helped him.

GOETHE   He had written poems; yes.
But if I helped at all it was to find
A tiny salary from the Duke's fund
For scientific purposes. We were
Fascinated by mosses, looked at seeds
Under his microscope.

SCHILLER   Well, the Professor
Seems, from this talk, to break all into
          fragments,
Which every Natural History lecturer
Does, who comes to his Society.

GOETHE   I can't bear dogs barking. Were you distracted?

SCHILLER   No.

GOETHE   But, Schiller, I agree with you:
All Nature's one, to me. Let's call it 'leaf':
A leaf that draws its moisture from the earth
We call a root. Expanded, it's a bulb.

Then it contracts to sprout up in a stem;
Expands to leaves, contracts to a green bud,
Expands again to flower, contracts to fruit –
Systole, diastole, like our heart,
The rhythm of all life – even the rocks
Which, over a vast time-scale, do the same.

SCHILLER   That's not a scientific observation!

GOETHE   *(Taken aback)* What is it, then?

SCHILLER   A concept, an idea!

GOETHE   *(Coldly)* Schiller, I'm very pleased to find I have
Ideas without my knowing it; can see
Yes, contemplate these 'ideas' with my eyes.

SCHILLER   It's strange you see the slow development
Of rocks, when by sudden catastrophe
Humanity evolves, as now in France.
Robespierre's volcano throws Napoleon
Like lava out to reshape Europe.

GOETHE   He
Is what I call demonic. Certain men –
Not always the most gifted, clever, kind
Or good – emanate a titanic force
That overwhelms even the elements.
Morality is powerless against
Such energy – incredible, till here
To sweep the world with bloodshed, far
    beyond
Notions of good and evil. Moralists
May brand him what they will. The masses,
    though,
Will follow such a magnet. Who can say
How far his influence extends? Just one
Is thrown up at one time. Nothing impedes
His onward progress but the universe
Itself, on which the demon declares war
Till all is left in ruins.

SCHILLER   Or reshaped
     Like landscapes after a volcano's calmed.

GOETHE   Etna I've seen; Stromboli; and I've trod
     Where Tartarus rolls flaming Phlegethon
     Hurling great boulders in its fiery current.
     Sea-water hitting burning coal-seams throws
     High the volcano's lava mushroom cloud.

SCHILLER   I've seen the strange contraption you have
       made
     To find colour's relation to the eye,
     But vertigo topples my giddying mind!

GOETHE   If light resolves itself to prismic colours,
     Then darkness, too, must also do the same.
     A white disc on a black ground gives the
       spectrum:
     A black disc on a white one does so, too!
     Colour is not contained in Mother Light
     (That's superstition, old, alchemical)
     But is the child of Darkness fused with Light.
     Many poets greater than myself
     Have lived, and will; but I am really proud
     To have found out the hidden truth of colour.
     I've published on this. Incredulity
     As to my competence is all I've won.

SCHILLER   Though from a distance, I have watched –
       seven years –
     The way your mind is journeying, a path
     That I increasingly admire, in awe.
     You see all as a unity, and find
     The key to knowledge starting from the
       simplest
     Seeds, up step by step to mankind: all-
     Embracing. The mind's most heroic quest,
     Far beyond one man's lifetime's compassing.
     Your mind's intuitive, and it creates
     Individuals, but such ones show

The features of their species. Mine is not.
It's speculative, rather – and my plays
Seem much more about types. Nature, to you
Reveals herself unpreconceived, to shape.
I begin with ideas. Both ways can meet
At centre, with integrity. If you
Will help me with a magazine I'm starting
Perhaps we might ...?

GOETHE   Since I returned to Weimar
All has seemed changed. I don't mind telling
          you
I have been lonely. I delay too long,
Hesitate to complete work; set aside
My *Faust*, for instance. You are impetuous:
Yet not the hot-head I had thought at first –
The youth who wrote *The Robbers*. After this
Unexpected encounter at a lecture
It seems we must continue on our search
Together. You thrill to philosophy.
I cannot come to terms with its dividing,
Separating. Spur my solitude;
And, if I can, I'll share my gratitude.

SCHILLER   Here is my house. Come in! I've poems, too,
Of a new poet, Hölderlin, to show you.
(I've sent copies to Herder.) I can't add
To your vast store of thought and knowledge,
          but
I'll run beside and urge you on to write.
Let's hammer out our differences; tonight!
(Exeunt)

SCENE FIVE

ANNA AMALIA, WIELAND, CHARLOTTE VON STEIN,
LOTTE SCHILLER *playing cards.*

AMALIA   My glass carriage is so small my crinoline
Hangs out the windows either side, and that

Is no way for Friedrich the Second's niece
To be seen by her subjects! I lead trumps.

WIELAND   Duchess Amalia ...

AMALIA   Dowager Duchess, please!
My son has a good Duchess in Luise:
A princess, like myself (Darmstadt, not
        Brunswick).
Her father, the Landgrave, at his spinet
Composed, with just two fingers, for his troops,
Military marches, catalogued with care:
Fifty-two thousand, three hundred, sixty-five!
Her mother, in their vault, dug her own grave
And by it, on a sun-shaft couch, would read.
I handed my dear son this government
When he was eighteen, twenty years ago
After Wieland had tutored him three years.
You had already translated Shakespeare
By then? I know you wrote some naughty
        poems!
Now; I must ask you all: what do you make
Of Goethe's *Roman Elegies,* just out
In the new magazine: *The Hours?* Are they
Truly Roman, copied from Propertius,
Or bedroom secrets of his flower-girl mistress?
All this about a 'rocking, creaking bed',
And 'your plain woollen dress slips to the floor',
Tapping his poem's metre on her back
While she sleeps in his arms!

WIELAND   I lead a club.
Horace himself confesses to such things,
And was attacked for copying the Greeks.
Goethe goes on: 'We don't kiss all the time;
We often share sound words of common-sense.'

CHARLOTTE   Ah! I can't bear it! Listen what Goethe wrote me:
'Dearest Angel, (seventh of June) when one
        loves

 One should tell everything and share together.
 Absence comes with the hose when fire's
            extinguished'.

WIELAND   Whatever does he mean? Honoured madam,
 The trouble is Germany, unlike France,
 Has no tradition of great literature.
 We have great cities, but are not a nation.
 All Athens went to watch their dramatists
 As drama and religion, civic pride,
 Were one. We're fragmented. Why even
            Shakespeare
 Was watched by Queen and *hoi polloi.* We have
 No public, only coteries, for the arts,
 So we must urge Schiller and Goethe on
 To breed a magazine that ploughs all fields,
 Knocks down the petty boundaries, dungs the
            soil
 Of national consciousness, to grow great works.

CHARLOTTE   I lead a heart. Spare me his "Roman" poems!
 They all shout of his Weimar Garden House
 Where round my sloping altar flowers wave.
 He's sailed to shipwreck on a South Sea
            nymph;
 But this friendship with Schiller, Lotte, might
 Begin to bring him home.

LOTTE   My husband, Fritz,
 Is like a boy unleashed – writes all the time
 To Goethe. They're composing epigrams
 Against their critics in an arrow shower:
 Four hundred, so far – all for publication.
 I'm afraid some will blow back in the wind.

CHARLOTTE   'Everything is so still, I hear my clock
 Ticking, the wind, and water in the distance.'
 That's what he wrote to me his first night in
 His Garden House. Now all we hear are bed-
            creaks.

Had he not left us for two years to strut
In Italy, the stealthy hand of Time
Might have escaped his notice on my cheeks.
He sees me as I am, a love grown old,
Past bearing age, a memory, a scold.

LOTTE   A spade. The crowing foot of Time claws all,
But as the maple turns to fiery gold
In autumn, far excelling modest spring,
We can enhance our leafy summer years
Teaching our children from experience.
My little son is not yet one year old,
But yours is your companion ... Herder!

Enter HERDER.

HERDER   Duchess? *(Bows)*
May I encroach? I thought that you should
     know
The news from France: Robespierre's been
     guillotined!
Let's hope his reign of blood and terror ends.

LOTTE   The Dowager stands up! She needs her friends.

LOTTE *goes over to help* AMALIA *and escort her out.*
Exeunt all except HERDER.

SCENE SIX

HERDER *and* HÖLDERLIN.

HERDER   Ah! Hölderlin. Welcome to Weimar! You,
I hear, in student days at Tübingen,
Shared a room with that thorough Jacobin
Hegel?

HÖLDERLIN   He was and is my friend.

HERDER   And are
          You with the Frau Charlotte von Kalb?

HÖLDERLIN   I am,
          Pastor Herder. Just now I'm alone.
          My friend Friedrich Stäudlin, and then Schiller
          Helped me become house-tutor to her son,
          Nine-year-old Fritz. Apart from a local parson,
          And Frau von Kalb's female companion – a
          Young lady of rare intellect and feeling:
          Wilhelmine Kirms – we're isolated;
          And often even Frau von Kalb's away.

HERDER   Schiller sent me your poems. Like you I am
          Sadly aware how far we lag behind
          Greece, in its golden age. Europe has had
          One glory, its own Middle Ages – times
          Of chivalry, of love and of religion:
          But not the classic form, the dignity,
          The swift, unerring, accurate perception
          All aeons must acknowledge was the Greeks'.

HÖLDERLIN My heart belongs already to the dead:
          My novel *Hyperion* ...

HERDER   And we must not
          (Forgive me; above all else I am a teacher)
          Allow nostalgia for what is ideal –
          And did exist in Athens – draw us from
          Our duties.

HÖLDERLIN   We can never recreate
          Those mighty works, but should acquire their
              spirit
          So future ages may assimilate
          Without nostalgia.

HERDER   Future? Past? The present!
          Here and now is where our duty lies!
          Goethe has made all of us skate on ice,

His fashion, on our specially flooded meadows
With glowing braziers, torches, fireworks!
Why, wrapped in furs on decorated sledges,
Masked ladies swirl the snow-ballroom for
    love.
Frau von Stein skated eight hours to its music.
On the ice, I explained my theory to him:
The genius of mankind blossoms, then moves
From one place in one epoch to another,
Across new dynasties, fresh generations.

HÖLDERLIN   But, like the spring, it moves from land to land.

HERDER   Decent, fulfilled humaneness, yes, for all,
Must be the art and whole aim of our race;
For if we fail, or slack our education,
Uncultured, brutish bestiality
Rides out to conquer. Every country must,
In its own different way, and style, strive for
The immortality Athens achieved.
It must be national: literature, the State,
Religion, politics, conventions, art,
All must have these two aims: a humane
    outlook,
Based on democratic self-definition,
Exchanging honour with far different nations;
Harmonious music of a world at peace.

HÖLDERLIN   What of Robespierre? The Terror now in
    France?

HERDER   I thought a golden age – this blossoming –
Had dawned in France. All the world's hopes
    were there.
The Reformation spread the clergy's riches;
This revolution could complete that work,
So every individual could vote
A voice in government – all run the State
And feudalism frost to sudden death.
But now this mad, demonic force unleashed

Shatters the grace and measure Greece
          upheld.

HÖLDERLIN   Germany, at the heart of Europe, could –
              No longer Europe's endless battleground –
              Flower through German youth and
                  womanhood,
              In peace, with patience, tolerance, hard work,
              Pindar's 'rare shining love of God and man'
              The Greek achievement in a German form.
              That tyrant Marat's slaughtered in his bath,
              And Robespierre's faced up to his guillotine:
              Pray to Christ that the moderate French may
                  win
              Whose cause is nothing less than Rights of Man.
              (Shyly) But do you like my poems?

HERDER   When they scan.
              (Exeunt)

                    SCENE SEVEN

          CHARLOTTE VON STEIN *and* GOETHE.

CHARLOTTE   You've read my letter?

GOETHE   Oh, belovèd, yes!
              At last we speak! No. I'll plead no excuse.
              But let me have your confidence once more!
              May we talk quietly, without emotion?

CHARLOTTE   Impossible.

GOETHE   Without ill-feeling, then?

CHARLOTTE   What can you say?

GOETHE   If you are suffering
              Because of me, then you must hurt me, too;
              But isn't it better we add up both sides

And leave inflicting pain – close the account?
And yet, in every bill, I am your debtor.
Dearest, let us forgive each other; now –
Rather than 'all', or 'nothing'. I have secrets
From Italy to share with you ...

CHARLOTTE   No; please!
I do not want to hear them. While away,
You had gone cold on all your friends; forgot
Our sacred date: the twelfth of November!

GOETHE   Why
Repulse my confidences, when for years
We shared all things however personal?
These mean a lot to me, and are important.

CHARLOTTE   I do not want to hear about your lust.

GOETHE   When I came back from Italy you'd changed.
The Duchess saves a seat for me, by Herder
Now! They set off for Venice. It goes empty
Because I have returned to be with you.

CHARLOTTE   You might as well have stayed in Italy.

GOETHE   Why so sarcastic?

CHARLOTTE   Why unsympathetic?

GOETHE   What do you mean?

CHARLOTTE   You know what I mean.

GOETHE   But you were moody before you had heard
Of Christiana.

CHARLOTTE   Please! Don't name the whore.

GOETHE   Though you have lost four daughters, you have
                three

Fine sons; your own sweet children. I have none.
Aged thirty-eight I saw, for the first time
An unclothed, loving woman – yes, in Rome!
You never let me feel you.

CHARLOTTE   My husband
Alone, as well you know, gives me my children.

GOETHE   Oh, don't you understand? So rarified
A spiritual love as you demanded –
Though quite the deepest of my life – could not
Prevent sweet Nature bursting through the
          poise.
You separated spirit from the body
Refining to abstraction our angelic
Harmony of souls. I skated; swam,
Even in December, naked in the Ilm;
Slept out of doors, rode from Leipzig to
          Weimar
In some eight hours to subdue and control,
To discipline myself. You were fulfilled.

CHARLOTTE   Didn't Euripides' Medea say
She'd rather face the forefront of the battle
Than bear a child?

GOETHE   But, my love, making seven!
Obsessive purity became my goal.
And now, although I'll gladly share all with you,
You will not listen: grudge, carp, turn away.

CHARLOTTE   You keep a whore.

GOETHE   She is not, nor has been.
Who else is hurt? Who else lays claim to her
Or to the hours I spend with her? No one.
Ask Fritz, your son; ask Herder, or his wife
Whether I'm less solicitous of friends
Or more, since knowing Christiana! If
You are the only one of all my friends

Who sees no warm improvement in me, why?
When I would talk, you shut my lips. When I
Enjoy my friends you complain of neglect.
You criticize (and make me ill-at-ease)
My looks, enthusiasms – even my movements!
And you don't listen when I say you drink
Far too much coffee. You know what ...

CHARLOTTE   No more!

GOETHE   Yes; we must write each other loving letters
             Now we have cleared the air a little.

CHARLOTTE   No.
             If you must write, then send a note to Fritz.
             My son adores you still; as I did, once.

GOETHE   Look at the moon! Our river! Both are full.
                 Bush and valley, moon, are yours
                     Silent through the mist.
                 You dissolve my heartbreak's cause
                     Where we once had kissed.

CHARLOTTE   Much-loved river, flow on now;
                     I'll no more delight.
                 Kisses, laughter, faithful vow
                     Die, full moon, tonight.

GOETHE   Something precious I possessed.
                     Now that time is past;
                 Yet it lingers in my breast
                     Hurting, holding fast.

CHARLOTTE   Sad and happy echoes brood
                     Still I must confess.
                 Mindlessly in solitude
                     Pace my loneliness.

Fade.

SCENE EIGHT

HERDER *and* GOETHE.

HERDER   In flies my woodpecker!

GOETHE   Of all my friends
You, who accepted my moon round your earth
In Strasbourg days, you understand me best.
Let us be what we are, and celebrate
The fact that we shall often disagree.
Why, you and I can stand a shock or two!
Speak out direct – malicious, serious –
All that you feel. We who aspire to fame
Undying should compel men to unleash
All that is belched and rumbled against us.
Our life, our work, our presence will absorb,
Purify and disarm such poisoned truths,
While what we learn from them will make us
          strong.

HERDER   Your *Wilhelm Meister* which you pressed on me
Is an immoral novel. Felix is Mariane's
Illegitimate product of a fling
Wilhelm had with the actress; and Mignon,
The child he buys from circus tight-rope
          dancers,
His loyal shadow, is the incest-fruit
Of his own harper you make kill himself.

GOETHE   But that is life; and art's integrity!

HERDER   The ethical must have priority
Over such self-indulgent aesthete's whims.

GOETHE   You, who love poetry, would act the censor.

HERDER   The fine arts regulate our loose desires,
Our fancies, as a lens distils out truth –

Known to us mortals only in reflection –
So, guided, harmonized by reason, souls
May shed all frivolous impurities,
And reflect back true goodness.

GOETHE   Schiller loves
To test experience by a moral standard.
I reserve judgement, write of what is there,
Destructive and creative: man's dark fire.

HERDER   I loathe that idol, the philosopher
That Schiller worships, mathematician Kant.

GOETHE   Immanuel Kant! You were his pupil once
At Königsberg.

HERDER   I was enthralled by him.
He taught me to probe basic principles,
But I'll scrub stains of his philosophy
From off the future's doorstep. How can he say
That man is evil? Schiller does not mind
That Kant 's destroying Christ's morality
And mortgaging past, present, to the future!
Mankind may be the bud which God creates
To flower after death in Paradise,
But buds need tenderness, and have their
        beauty.

GOETHE   Why are you jealous of my younger friend
Schiller?

HERDER   You were my young friend I taught,
But he's perverting you.

GOETHE   He tests my thought.

SCENE NINE

KLEIST, WILHELMINE *and* LUISE VON ZENGE.

KLEIST

Come in, Wilhelmine von Zenge, and
Your golden sister, Luise. Don't think of me
Just as the boy next door – your twenty-two-
Year-old ex-Prussian guardsman, Heinrich von
    Kleist,
Who fought Napoleon (I was sixteen
An ensign in the Army of the Rhine)
But as 'Professor' Kleist. I've had this lectern
Specially constructed to teach you. Sit down.
I stand behind it. Pay attention. Your
Ethical improvement is my aim.

LUISE

Where are the other ten who should be here?

KLEIST

All in good time. You have least far to walk.

LUISE

You hammered on our door lest we forgot!

KLEIST

Enough! Pupils don't answer back. Spelling,
Grammar, and History of Civilization
Is my course for you.

WILHELMINE

                                        Is that wide enough?

KLEIST

Be quiet! Here is a copy of *Wallenstein*
By Friedrich Schiller. You must study it;
Study, not merely read it! Now – Thought
    Problems
To give parade drill to your misty minds.
Answer the following on your note-pads. One:
'Which is better – to be good or do good?'
Two: 'In marriage does husband or the wife
Lose more by loss of the other?' Go on! Write!
Three: 'May the wife inspire the deep affection
Of no-one but her husband?' Luise! *(Slams book*

shut) Right!
I do not ask you here into my house,
My guardian Aunt's own rooms, for you to
    stare
Out of the window! Go back home at once!

Exit LUISE.

Now Wilhelmine: here, corrected, are
Your exercises.

*Wilhelmine rises, comes to his lectern and accepts not
only her corrected exercises but an envelope.*

WILHELMINE   Thank you. What is this?
An envelope for me?

KLEIST   It is.

WILHELMINE   Red ink!
You've found enough mistakes to take away
My confidence!

KLEIST   There's only right and wrong
In composition.

WILHELMINE   *(Reads letter)* Kleist. I can't believe it!
You ask my hand in marriage?

KLEIST   Yes, I do
With tears in eyes. Please sit down. Will you
    write
Down your ideal of what a husband is?
Then how far I approximate to it?
Am I not noble?

WILHELMINE   Really!

KLEIST   Then describe
The happiness that you anticipate

From such a marriage.

WILHELMINE   What do you expect?

KLEIST   A girl I can improve. Whatever her
                Accomplishments, if she cannot be taught
                She's not for me as I myself must mould her.

WILHELMINE   Reverse Pygmalion – woman into art!

KLEIST   And will you keep this secret from your
                            parents?

WILHELMINE   No, I will not. Kleist, you are not at all
                My idea of a husband.

                Re-enter LUISE.

LUISE   May I? Sorry!

KLEIST   Have you been standing out there all the time?

LUISE   I'm afraid I heard all.

KLEIST   Then plead for me,
                Luise. I play the flute and clarinet.
                What can be her objection to me? Eh?

LUISE   One is, this is abrupt. Another one
                Our parents will spell out is that you have
                No job, no suitable employment: just
                A toy professor 's inadmissable.

KLEIST   I've had six years of army discipline,
                Garrison life – a Prussian officer ...

LUISE   And we all know you resigned your commission
                To be a student. You've angered the King

With your petition for discharge. A student!
Where, may we ask?

KLEIST   Knowledge is universal.
I'll leave tomorrow for Berlin.

WILHELMINE   Take this
(Pulls off her locket and gives it to Kleist)
You mad, impetuous, mercurial
Ex-soldier. In it is a minature
Of me, and a lock of my hair. Send word
From Berlin what you do to earn a living,
And see if the von Zenges are forgiving.

SCENE TEN

GOETHE *'s house.*
CHRISTIANA, GOETHE *and* SCHILLER.

CHRISTIANA   Here, Privy-Councillor, is your best wine
For Herr Professor Schiller. Will you need
Some food?

GOETHE *asks* SCHILLER *with his eyes.* SCHILLER
declines.

GOETHE   No, thank you, Christiana.

Exit CHRISTIANA.

SCHILLER   She
Addresses you as Councillor in bed?

GOETHE   *(Laughs)* My small Erotikon, companion, friend,
I have dug up, transplanted with her roots
(Step-sister, brother, aunt), into my garden.
She brings me joy, her body in its splendour,
And cheerful peace.

SCHILLER   'Professor Schiller' too!
                        I like her accent: broad Thuringian.
                        Tell her I have declined the offer of
                        Chair of Philosophy at Tübingen.

GOETHE   Herder, who sneers you are a Kantian
                        Corrupting morals, will rejoice!

SCHILLER   Oh no,
                        You're wrong. Hear how his letter sings my
                                praises:
                        'The ideas you develop are profound
                        And lofty. They light up the goal to which
                        Each and all of us strive. Such radiance
                        Calls blessing from your readers for such
                                hope.'

GOETHE   Good God! Herder's a complex man!

SCHILLER   Sometimes
                        His venom against Kant's philosophy,
                        And your book *Wilhelm Meister*, 's like a dog
                        Sinking its fangs into an athlete's leg:
                        A powerful ally, but a mongrel, too,
                        Evacuating his unhealthiness
                        On us, yet never cured. But here is praise!
                        What did you think of Hölderlin's two poems?

GOETHE   'An den Äther' and 'Der Wanderer'?
                        I was not wholly unimpressed.

SCHILLER   They seem
                        To me too much like my own earlier stuff,
                        Impetuous in subjectivity.
                        Living as tutor in a merchant's house
                        He's thrown back on himself.

GOETHE   Yes, there's the milk
                        From your style's breast, but not your depth
                                and force.

The elements of poetry are there,
And a warmth, sweetness, temperateness too,
That are attractive. He should try an idyll,
And create human beings convincingly.

SCHILLER   Would he have been so subjective, extreme,
Idealistic, anyway? Or has
Loneliness, lack of poets' nourishment
And influence distorted balanced art?

GOETHE   So many gifted poets bite the frost –
Look at disquieting, acid, morbid Kleist!

Enter CHRISTIANA.

CHRISTIANA   Excuse me, Privy-Councillor, Professor,
But theatre-stuff and actors have arrived
With baggage and some children. They must not
Disturb you.

GOETHE   Settle them, then take some dancing.
(She loves to dance and tease – I like her to.)
Christiana, in our theatre
When personal relationships need oil
You are the perfect diplomatic cook.

SCHILLER   Irons out their problems as she presses shirts.

GOETHE   And both of us are unrepentant flirts.

Fade as CHRISTIANA *clears table.*

SCENE ELEVEN

SCHILLER *and* HÖLDERLIN; GOETHE *in the
background.*

SCHILLER   Ah, Hölderlin! Come in! Hölderlin – Goethe!

(HÖLDERLIN *gives a perfunctory wave, not having
caught* GOETHE*'s name.* GOETHE, *with a smile,
slowly waves back; not being accustomed to such curt
notice, and rather enjoying it*)
What can you tell me of your tutorship
I fixed for you with Frau von Kalb's son, Fritz?

HÖLDERLIN   I thought you knew: I've been sacked.

SCHILLER   Sacked?
                    But why?
              Charlotte is not unkind.

HÖLDERLIN   That's true: she's not.
              She gave me three months' wages so I could
              Settle in Jena where the writers are.
              She wrote a letter to my mother, too,
              Full of sweet fragrant herbs of reassurance.

SCHILLER   Why? What went wrong? Surely the pregnancy
              Of her friend, widow Wilhelmine Kirms,
              Is not your lusty legacy?

HÖLDERLIN   Susceptible –
              Where loveliness enfolds intelligence –
              To the mild scent breathed by proximity
              Of petalled hours alone where warm log fires,
              Candlelit eyes, once children are in bed,
              And storm wind whisper all the house is ours,
              I lived beside this tender Dresden girl –
              Hurt by her cruel husband and dark mother –
              And watched the flush of happiness return
              Like spring down through her neck while we
                    spoke low
              Practising French and reading scenes from
                    plays
              To improve our accents. She's one of the best
              Of all her sex: and was one cause I left.

SCHILLER   Well, did you need another?

HÖLDERLIN   It began well.
The boy was lovable, even angelic:
Pretty, honest, endlessly warm-hearted
And did what he was told. But all went wrong.
Gentleness had to yield to rod and shout.

SCHILLER   But why?

HÖLDERLIN   Why? Adolescence. Wicked evil.
I watched him day and night, leadenly tired
Sitting beside him till he fell asleep;
Pleading, or threatening, if his hand once
                    strayed,
To cure him of the habit; beating him
If I found he had done, or caught him at it.

SCHILLER   Well! Well! Poor Fritz! Here is my magazine
Thalia with your poem to Fate in it
Together with part of your *Hyperion* –
The first five letters of your novel. All
This issue else is written by myself.

HÖLDERLIN   Living close to great thinkers, men whose bold
Independent spirits beacon out,
Depresses and exalts: I flow and ebb.

SCHILLER   Send me more contributions by July.
And I commission you to translate Ovid's
Phaeton. You'll learn through that to curb
Your German vice, prolixity: one good
Idea diluted in a flood of verse.
I have some good news for you. Bear with me.
I'll be back in a moment. (*Exit* SCHILLER)

Long, awkward pause. GOETHE *slowly comes
downstage to* HÖLDERLIN *and picks up the copy of
'Thalia'.*

GOETHE   This is yours. (*Hands him 'Thalia'*)

HÖLDERLIN   Yes. (*Pause*)

GOETHE   How is Frau von Kalb?

HÖLDERLIN   Oh, never mind all that.

GOETHE   *(Amused)* You admire Schiller!

HÖLDERLIN   A soul of genius, breathtaking; sublime!
              The only man to whom I yield my freedom.

GOETHE   His influence will, if you let it, groom
              And help mature your gifts to excellence.

              Enter SCHILLER.

SCHILLER   Here is a contract with the publisher
              Cotta, for your *Hyperion*. I told him
              That you had a fair bit of genius
              And I will hope to shape it.

HÖLDERLIN   How can I thank you?
              Because I feel how much a word from you
              Decides my fate, to write I turn away.
              Sometimes, just to protect my freedom, I
              Wrestle in secret with your genius;
              And if at times I seem distracted when
              We meet, Schiller, it is because I fear
              Your total domination of my mind
              Till diffidence – timidity – kills art.
              I'm jumpy in your presence: servile, defiant:
              Equilibrium flies off like a duck
              From my small pool of ink. Imperious
              Masterpieces humble me till I'm
              A boy against a grown man.

GOETHE   So we feel
              Measured beside the ancient world.

HÖLDERLIN   *(Abruptly)* Too true.
              Who is not prostrated, face down, before
              The terrible splendour of the Ancient World

That forest hurricane tearing up young trees
Grasping control of his imagination,
Especially when he lacks, as I do, strength –
And confidence of self identity.

SCHILLER   Have you a job to go to?

HÖLDERLIN   Yes. I hope
The Frankfurt banker Jakob Gontard will
Employ me as house-tutor for his son,
Eight-year-old Henry.

SCHILLER   Well; a second chance.
Beware the French in Frankfurt! What's the pay?

HÖLDERLIN   Four hundred gulden yearly, and all found.

SCHILLER   Make sure no lady's stomach there grows round!

SCENE TWELVE

JAKOB GONTARD *holding a testimonial,* SUSETTE
GONTARD, HÖLDERLIN.

GONTARD   Friedrich Hölderlin, I'm pleased to meet you!
This is Susette, my wife – a Borkenstein,
Now mother of my four children. The eldest
    one,
Henry, is eight years old (the others are girls).
He needs a tutor, and I see you are
A friend of Hegel, Schelling, from the same
Tübingen Seminary, destined for
A country parish, perhaps?

HÖLDERLIN   Well ... thank you sir;
But all my thoughts are finishing my novel.

SUSETTE   I've read the part published in Schiller's *Thalia,*
And loved it.

GONTARD   You two are much the same age,
And should get on. I'm a banker. For me
Business comes first. You can talk about art,
And music, to her – and my little boy?

HÖLDERLIN   I play the flute ...

GONTARD   Madam Gontard the piano!
I've bought some etchings of the painter
        Titian's
Work, which you must go through and explain.
One thing we all should know: Napoleon,
Not content with firing his cannon balls
On Frenchmen surrounding the National
        Convention
In Paris, crosses the river Lahn with his
Great army. If he threatens Frankfurt, I
Shall stay, but you all go to Bad Driburg
To take the peaceful waters on your own
Until this flood of refugees has passed.
Susette – I'll leave you two to winnow details.
(HÖLDERLIN *bows. Exit* GONTARD)

SCENE THIRTEEN

SUSETTE   Friedrich, I hear that Goethe is in town
And visited your friend Schiller this morning.

HÖLDERLIN   Why, *I* was there – oh no! No! Was that Goethe?

SUSETTE   What wasp has stung your brain?

HÖLDERLIN   Horror's panic.
Schiller told him my name; and told me his –
But I was so preoccupied with Schiller
I didn't catch it; scarcely looked at him.
He hardly spoke, until, for a short time,
Schiller left us alone, and he leafed through
My fragment of *Hyperion* in *Thalia*.

I blushed to a plum red, so when he asked
After the Frau von Kalb I brushed him off
Curtly, with coldness quite unlike me. Had
I known that it was Goethe, I'd have paled
Into a corpse! Oh what a hideous blunder!
Dismissed him on first meeting him. Disaster!

SUSETTE   Ah!
Your bruised emotions need my healing
          plaster. (*Exeunt*)

SCENE FOURTEEN

WIELAND, GOETHE *and* HERDER.

WIELAND   I learned some details of your illness, Goethe,
From prayers at our Masonic Lodge. Herder
Was present, too. Are you restored?

GOETHE   Nearly.
As you can see, my left eye's open now.
The tumour on my head and neck did not
Attack the brain. The cough and fever's
          cleared –
At last I can sleep lying down. Thank you
Good friends for all your kindnesses, and care.

HERDER   The slackening of our fibres, after fifty,
Reminds us everything is vanity;
And even friendship, noblest bond of men,
Manures in rotting decayed, human flesh.

GOETHE   The dung of illness sharpens new delight
In family and loved ones. Had I died,
August, my son, who'll soon be thirteen, would
Never perhaps have been confirmed. Will you,
Dear friend, who taught me how to see the
          Bible

As National poetry, yet gold for all,
Prepare my son in our own, liberal way
For his fresh first communion?

HERDER   Yes, I shall.
Since you spent six months with me in
          Strasbourg
So many years ago, I've hoped for this.
Now that Napoleon has signed the Peace
Of Lunéville, and France and Austria
Confirm in deepest vows their friendship over
The putrid corpses, we can hope your son
Will transcend habit, prejudice, and greed,
Self-interest, empty honour, indulgence,
And sensuality – those slave-chains we
Eagerly grasp – and hear the truth of God,
Before presumption pulls down punishment.
May poetry, flower of the human heart
And universal language of all time,
Expressing mankind's longing hopes, ideals
Beyond philosophy and history,
From its high stem be plucked by your young
          son.

Exit HERDER.

WIELAND   I'm glad the breach between you two is healed.

GOETHE   I've longed for this. He quarrelled with the Duke
And overwork, as new Vice-President
Of Consistory earned him rheumatic illness.
'I came to you in Weimar and turned down
A Göttingen professorship; and look
How I am treated! Fund-starved.' There was
          wrong
On both sides: crushed between them I was
          bruised.

WIELAND   I must leave now. Young Kleist waits at my
          home

Where two of my three single daughters dote
On him: Karoline and Luise ...

GOETHE   Who's just fourteen?

WIELAND   Yes. Luise deeply loves him; but Amalie,
Eighteen, 'hates' (she says) the Prussian poet.
She is afraid of falling for him, too!
He is a genius; yet he's odd at meals.
We've given him a room in which to write,
But when he joins us for the midday meal
He mumbles, like a madman, to himself
Between his chewing teeth. He joins our talk,
Then suddenly, because some word's been said,
Falls silent, abstracted; and starts his mumbling.

GOETHE   Have you peered in his mind with gentle
                questions?

WIELAND   I have. I told him when he eats with us
We don't want mouse-droppings instead of
                pepper.
He was acutely upset, and explained
His tragedy, half-written, is inspired
At times by odd words which he must work up
There and then. He will write a scene, then
                burn it!
'Do what I do.' I said. 'Draft the whole play,
Then go back and rework the details.' 'You
Are fluent. I must perfect every speech
Before I move on: but so often then
I lose my links.' 'What you call fluency
Is only won after innumerable
Drafts are wrestled with. Catch the winged
                words
While they sport in imagination's sky
Sun-blest by inspiration!' 'But my pen'
Kleist answered, 'flimsies out my deepest
                thoughts.
What I conceive is never brought to birth.'

GOETHE   You'll guide him to great poets of the past.
           I'll tell you something as we part. I have
           Shakespeare in three translations: Eschenburg's
           Literal version; Schlegel's romantic one;
           But I prefer – even though some is changed –
           Your own. Make sure I meet eccentric Kleist!
           We need new plays of quality.

WIELAND   I shall!

                      SCENE FIFTEEN

           AMALIE WIELAND, KAROLINE WIELAND, LUISE
           WIELAND *and* KLEIST.

AMALIE   Why did you leave our brother on his own
           In Erfurt?

KLEIST   Amalie; we waited. He
           Searched a past girl-friend and fell in her arms.
           We blew our nails in the cold.

AMALIE   Our Ludwig wrote
           To father all about you.

KLEIST   What did he tell?
           How we were reprimanded by police
           Because he laughed and pulled a comic face
           When ordered to leave Bern within twelve
               hours?
           They cut that down to three; and then one hour!
           We nearly lost our chance.

LUISE   He said you are
           Greater than any German dramatist
           Till now! Please will you take this
               handkerchief?
           You see I have embroidered strawberries
           For you.

KLEIST   Like Desdemona! Are you jealous?
No need. I've written to my fiancée
Wilhelmine: 'I have many worries.
Dear girl, please don't write to me any more.
(LUISE *elated*)
I have no other wish than to die soon.'
(LUISE *deflated*)

LUISE   How could you? When you know I'll decorate
Every one of your hankies; pillowcases ...

KAROLINE You break your own engagement and a heart
So brutally? You, whom women adore,
Must treat emotions gently – not least ours.

LUISE   Heine, I cannot bear it when you talk
Of death. You are so vulnerable, so strange ...
(*Weeps*)

KAROLINE See? You are upsetting all the household,
Letting her give her all while you, detached,
Confuse her feelings. Please don't break her
    heart.

AMALIE   Only fourteen; but she's a woman who
Is hopelessly in love with you. Please leave
If you cannot respond. Visit our father,
But end this garden greenhouse atmosphere.

KAROLINE There comes a time when those who love you
    most
Can bear your company, so self-absorbed,
No longer. We three girls have washed your
    clothes,
Hung them to dry where all the world may see.
Please let the scandal die, and leave us be?

    Fade.

SCENE SIXTEEN

SUSETTE *playing the piano,* HÖLDERLIN *the flute.*

SUSETTE
It's the new work by Ludwig van Beethoven:
His flute sonata in B flat. Do you like it?
His style's improved since he left Bonn to live
In Joseph Haydn's Vienna. It's brought
        problems,
Though. Viennese pianists are quick
To ape his mannerisms, and write down –
As their own – his brilliant improvisations.
As a result, he's rushing into print
Variations on Mozart's 'Se vuol ballare',
Fourteen variations in E flat,
And other improvisations on the piano ...
Why are you crying?

HÖLDERLIN
                    Cloudy music fills,
Dampens, my eyes. My dear friend and
        support,
Gotthold Friedrich Stäudlin, who urged me
To be a poet, has just drowned himself
Under the lapping waters of the Rhine.

SUSETTE
But why?

HÖLDERLIN
        Ah, why? He was a lyric poet
And revolutionary publisher.
He was expelled as *enragé* because
His sympathies were with the rebel French.
Oh, Madam Gontard, please forgive me! Like
Those clouds, up there, that cross the peaceful
        moon,
I shall drift on, and your full, honey light
Suspended still, will gleam – forgetting this –
In all your beauty as before.

SUSETTE
                    Suicide

Of a friend is enough to cloud our sun
And stamp fresh furrows on God's patient face.
But ... is there something else? How can I help?

HÖLDERLIN   Perhaps by listening. Madam Gontard ...

SUSETTE   Susette
When we're alone.

HÖLDERLIN   All right. I'll try. Susette.
But may I ask your privacy, that you
Hold to yourself the secret I shall tell
If I confide in you?

SUSETTE   Friedrich, yes.
No word of ours will be profaned beyond
This skin-tight door that locks it to my breast.

HÖLDERLIN   When I was tutor to Charlotte von Kalb's
Young Fritz, for many weeks I lived alone
(Save for the children and the servants) in
Their remote manor-house at Waltershausen –
Stäudlin, through Schiller, found the job for
    me.
I say 'alone'; except for a young widow,
Charlotte's companion, Wilhelmine Kirms.
The parson called her 'rare in intellect
And sensibility'. She bore my child –
Louise Agnese; and I have just heard
That little daughter, scarcely one year old,
Has died of smallpox.

SUSETTE   When the hammer blows
Of fate select us for their anvil, our
White heat of grief supples us lest we break;
And tears are due, both to the friend, and babe.
Yes, let them flow.

HÖLDERLIN   You gaze on in your beauty
And have not grown too proud to comfort me.

SUSETTE   Come! We shall go, perhaps with Wilhelm
                        Heinse,
                And my friend Marie Rätzer – I suppose
                She is my Wilhelmine! – to the museum
                With its Greek statues, to the Art Gallery ...

HÖLDERLIN   You, with your Titianesque complexion
                Have won your husband's gift of fresh
                        engravings
                Of that great painter.

SUSETTE   Shall we look through
                        those Titians?
                (She takes up an etching and shares it.
                Show slide of 'Shepherd and Nymph' (1575/1576)
                Vienna, Kunsthistorisches Museum)
                A shepherd plays a flute to a bare nymph
                Half-turned away, lying upon a fur,
                The neck of the skinned animal held down
                By her soft, honeyed thighs. She looks
                        around
                As music ceases from the oaten pipe.

HÖLDERLIN   Look at the very centre of this picture.
                It is a hand caressing her right arm,
                But not the flute-player's, nor is it hers
                As she is nude, and the hand wears a cuff.

SUSETTE   Whose is it then?

HÖLDERLIN   The painter's. He's in love
                With his voluptuous creation, like
                Pygmalion. This disembodied feel
                Scratches her placid plumpness, which exists
                Solely to be inspected; available,
                Exhibited to all, but by none touched.

SUSETTE   The half-stilled music of his fingered flute
                Should call us back, now that your tears have
                        dried,

To our own flute sonata. What is this?
*(Takes another etching. Show slide of 'Venus with
Organist and Cupid' (1548) Madrid, Prado)*

HÖLDERLIN   Everything 's for our pleasure. Here she lies,
The mistress, undressed, turned towards us, as
A cupid whispers in her ear. While she's
Distracted from the music, unashamed,
Lying on velvet in a lovers' garden
Where trees recede in perspective to gold,
The organ player turns round to the nude
And gazes at her hair not on her head.

SUSETTE   In some ways it is she who is like you:
Self-defined, entirely herself,
Regardless of spectators, morals, laws –
Just intimacy of transparent truth.
It's that attracts a woman.

HÖLDERLIN   Is that true?
*(Show slide of 'Venus of Urbino' (1538) Florence,
        Uffizi)*
Look here at this Urbino Venus. We
Intrude upon her naked intimacy,
And yet she is not fazed, rocking herself.
She knows we watch, yet does not frown, or
        smile.
Her gesture is the sum of all her life's
Dreams, secrets, explorations, happiness,
Those hidden thoughts savoured so deep,
        alone.
We thrill in having caught her: unsurprised,
She knows her private secret now is ours
And likes our joy in accepting her gift,
Now we're in on her secret, discovered.
Her pleasure deepens as her glow shines from
Ours – the spectators' – eyes.

SUSETTE   I feel her eyes,
Her palpable immediacy set

Off by her ear-ring, the immortal jewel
Against her fleeting, private, youth-flushed
            flesh,
Mocking mortality. *(Taking another etching. Show*
slide of 'Mary Magdalene' (1535) Florence,
Pitti Palace)   Here Magdalene
Presses warm fingers through hair to her breast.

HÖLDERLIN   Furs, skins of animals, dogs, curls and forests,
Gardens in which the intimate's refined
To what's most private, hidden: this invites,
So Titian seems to say. His mastery
Sweeps away everything not secret, true,
Virgin, never seen but ever there.
(Show slide of 'Lucretia' (1523) Hampton Court)
He tears away the veil from Eden's fall
And all its consequent hypocrisies
And violates back to unfiltered sight,
Filling each warm nude out from her inside
Through fullness to skin-shadowed sunlight till
We live more fully knowing whence we came.

SUSETTE   *(Show slide of 'Venus Anadyomene' (1519/1525)*
Edinburgh, National Gallery of Scotland)
We are attracted when we come upon –
Surprised – a true original: like us,
But other. What is sensuality
But radiance contained in private gift,
Caught, then submitted – like a wayward
            curl.

HÖLDERLIN   Titian loves moss, and coiffures. Hair
            becomes
For him the crowning glory of our fall.
It can be lifted, burrowed into, pulled,
Brushed, parted, dampened, stroked, but
            never shaved
So it won't grow again. It's our last thread
With Paradise.

SUSETTE   *(Taking another etching. Show slide of 'Death of*
               Actaeon' (1562) London, National Gallery)
                          The fig splits open with
               Ripeness of its own bursting energy,
               And desire quivers like an arrow shot
               Into that sunburned oak that welcomes it.
               (Takes another. Show slide of 'Venus and Adonis'
               (1553/ 1554) Madrid, Prado)
               Here naked Venus, asking to be pressed,
               Only her hair full-dressed, impulsively
               Clings her arms round departing, clothed
                    Adonis.
               Her awkwardness brings her startlingly present.
               You, who know women so well; so detached
               Yet vulnerable, spiritually undimmed,
               May draw me if you wish.

HÖLDERLIN   No, not Susette:
               My name for you shall be Socrates' muse –
               Diotima. Rich in your unique spirit
               Unmatched, your own, like delicate blossoms
                    in winter
               Searching for sun, you stay loyal to your
               Own childhood's essence, facing another world
               Yet capable in this.

SUSETTE   Yes, you may kiss.   *(Fade.)*

                            SCENE SEVENTEEN

               GOETHE*'s house.*
               GOETHE, SCHILLER *and* KLEIST.

SCHILLER   So Kleist pays us a visit? Wieland writes:
               'If Aeschylus and Sophocles and Shakespeare
               Collaborated on a tragedy
               The play might be Kleist's *Death of Guiscard the*
                    Norman.'

GOETHE   Only a fragment of that play is written
                As yet.

SCHILLER   So Wieland says: 'If all the rest
                Is as the part Kleist read to me, then he
                Will fill the gaps Goethe and Schiller leave
                In our new park of German Literature.'

GOETHE   Lotte von Kalb also admires Kleist's work.

SCHILLER   What do you think?

GOETHE   I am prepared to like him.
                He seems entirely given to contradiction
                Worked through with morbid, systematic skill.
                He takes the ugly, the disquieting
                In nature, but ingenious thoroughness
                Does not make up for a swift-moving plot.
                His Prussic acid corrodes his great gifts.

SCHILLER   The subjects lack all taste: a marquise made
                Pregnant while she's unconscious ...

GOETHE   An Amazon
                 On stage with one breast missing, reassuring
                The audience all her emotions are
                Still in the one remaining ...

SCHILLER   How repulsive!

                KLEIST *knocks at the door.*

GOETHE   Heinrich von Kleist, our poet. Come in!
                    Welcome!
                Wieland speaks well of you.

KLEIST   Goethe, it was
                The proudest moment in my life when he
                Beside his glowing fire at Ossmannstedt
                Listened as I read out *Guiscard the Norman*

(The little that I've written). I fell down
Before him at the close, and in the smoky
Candlelight covered his ancient hands
With hot and fervent kisses. We were speechless.

SCHILLER   What are you writing, apart from *The Norman?*

KLEIST   Schiller, I wrestle with that towering text
And find it throws me on the floor. I have
Something, Goethe, that I offer you
In homage on the bare knees of my heart.

GOETHE   A play? *(Takes it)*

KLEIST   It is.

GOETHE   *(Looks at it)* The Broken Water-Pitcher'.
Heine, I'm touched. I'll tell you what I'll do:
Study it, and – if it is actable –
I shall direct it on our stage myself.

SCHILLER   One can't ask more than that!

KLEIST   You are the new Messiah of the Arts!
Sometimes I feel my own work 's wretched trash
Beside your plays, and Schiller's; but they're mine –
Deformed, aborted children, but my own!
If you adopt this play, it's one more strike
Against those apes of reason the slick French.
We quarry our human emotions deep.
They glitter with the surface, not the truth.

GOETHE   Truth is a torch, but it's a monstrous one
That makes us turn away, blink, lest we burn.

KLEIST   From you two there is nothing I can't learn.

Exeunt.

SCENE EIGHTEEN

SUSETTE, HÖLDERLIN *and* JAKOB GONTARD.

SUSETTE

My husband wants to see you. Just be calm.
I know you love me, as I love you, too,
And that great gift cannot be stripped from
     me.
The immortal threads that bind us are grown
     from
All that is good, and beautiful, and strong
Beyond defeat in this world, though I know
The insults of the world will overwhelm
Us if we take each insult to the heart.
Yet, dearest, the keen wind of suffering
In absence from you will frost-bite my life.
So listen. If he forces you away ...

HÖLDERLIN

Is that his wish? Frostbite? I feel I am
A man more battered, bruised, destructible
Than most – shipwrecked, sea-buried with a
     weight
Roped round me to drag down my gasping
     mind.

SUSETTE

Yet keep your equilibrium, my love;
There are not many like you – though all say
You look my brother's twin.

HÖLDERLIN

                              How can a man
Forcing his passage through life's hostile
     crowds
Who shove, and rock him to and fro, who
     punch
And trip, retain his serene grace and poise?
Fate soils our purest hopes; our innocence
Coarsely corrupts in waves of tragedy.
For years I'm battered in so many ways –
And yet, I will be calm.

Enter JAKOB GONTARD.

GONTARD

Hölderlin.

HÖLDERLIN

Sir.

SUSETTE

Jakob, shall I stay?

GONTARD

You stay right here.
Hölderlin, I am told, from many mouths,
'Frau Gontard spends all morning in the study
Or in the summerhouse with Hölderlin.'
I know a house-tutor must enter in
To the domestic hearth to teach the child,
But Frankfurt's gossip blasts a deaf man's ear;
And I, though often absent, hear quite well.

SUSETTE

Jakob, what do you want? Don't taunt the man.

GONTARD

Taunt? Is a patient banker, trained to judge
Coolly the destinies of broken men
Likely to do more than enquire the truth?

HÖLDERLIN

Sir, I will do whatever you command.

GONTARD

I like you. Nearly two years you have been
Part of our family. I cannot thrill
My wife's intelligence with music, arts,
Poetry, and the tapestries of spirit.
That's not my world; and I'm aware of it –
Too, too aware I cannot meet her there!
You can, and do; but Susette is my wife,
The mother of my children, and my joy.
She knows my limitations, and that I
Do all I can to give security
To each of us – yes, you too – with hard cash
Earned over absences and night-lamp oil.
When I am tired, and very far from home,
Wondering why bald figures claim my days
Sapping vitality for means, not ends,

I think of her, my little ones, our home
Safe for return. I think of other things:
Of love, where, like a trusted thief crept in
Safe vaults, whose skill unpicks the secret lock
Of the most precious treasure in the world,
Is left bare emptiness where once was all.

HÖLDERLIN   The painful moment when we say 'Good-bye'
To some place where our hopes had bred fresh
    flowers
And ripened fruits till friends grew strong in
    joy
Is our foretaste of that cold ferryman
Whose payment is the colours of the earth.

GONTARD   Without my loved ones, why, what is life worth?
(Exit)

SUSETTE   Oh love! *(They embrace)* You were so fine.
Look! While we yet have time, listen to me.
Let's meet on the first Thursday of each month
(Unless the weather's foul, in which case come
The next – always a Thursday, so we know).
I'll be upstairs, as from my window I
Can see the poplar trees near where the hedge
Dips down. Stand there just as the clocks strike
    ten.
Put your stick on your shoulder as a sign.
I'll dust with a white cloth, and if I close
The window it's a sign I'm coming down:
But if I leave it open, all's not safe.
Go to the drive behind the summer house
And we'll exchange our letters through the
    hedge,
But mind the ditch! If anything goes wrong,
Try the same time next day. Let's each keep
    journals
Of all we think and do while we're apart,
Then pass them to each other. In this way
Our tears of grief will keep love from decay.

HÖLDERLIN   Oh, loving guardian spirit, when I'm far
             From you, death's angels will unstring my heart
             Of melody; yet all my life and art
             In absence I'll pour out to your bright star
             Breaking my darkness. You illumine all
             My nights and days. I'll come though blizzards
                 fall.

                        SCENE NINETEEN

             ANNA AMALIA, CHARLOTTE VON STEIN, LOTTE, *and*
             THUSNELDA *(hunchback maid).*

AMALIA   That upstart consul, Buonaparte, has signed
             At Amiens a treaty with Great Britain ...

CHARLOTTE   The British will not keep it. Who forgets
             How he sailed out from Toulon in French pride
             To conquer Egypt only to be sunk
             By Nelson at the battle of the Nile?
             The British win their wars.

AMALIA   We sent Herr Goethe
             To Switzerland, the Bern republic, to
             Negotiate a loan of fifty thousand
             Thaler against our collateral
             Of part of my estates, to help this country.
             Bern's cornucopia of bankers' gold
             Was drunk, raped, ransacked by Napoleon
             To the last glowing vault to finance his
             Egyptian expedition.

LOTTE   We were lucky
             Bern gold had reached us through the
                 Frankfurt fair.

AMALIA   Oh, I love fairs – it's in the Brunswick blood –
             When I can step aside from State affairs!
             Meanwhile dear Wieland teaches me Old Greek

And gives me fun with Aristophanes.

LOTTE   The bawdy Aristophanes!

AMALIA   Why, yes!
But I can see myself in Roman terms,
Too. Hear what I've translated from
          Propertius.
No, not his sexual escapades, but his
Ideal Patrician Matron's final words:

                    My innocence was yours alone
                              Husband. From wedding flame
                    To funeral brand and unburned bone
                              No accusations shame.
                    My house was noble. Nature gave
                              Me laws which I obeyed.
                    Married to one alone, I'm brave
                              To face Dis unafraid.
(Applause)
But Lotte, you sailed near the gates of death
And Dis's Kingdom, with the birth of your
Caroline.

LOTTE   I was delirious,
Like a drunk ship tossing between the days
And nights. Only my mother and my husband
Could I bear near me. Then you, Charlotte,
          took
Me in your home, and cared for me as though
I were your dying child.

AMALIA   *(To* CHARLOTTE*)* Your stoic strength
Turned the dark ship to steer back into light.

CHARLOTTE   The loss of my long intimacy with
Herr Goethe steels my heart against all hurt
And sorrows that may be in store for me.
That gives me strength. You would have nursed
          me, too,

Lotte. I can endure, and can forgive
Everything.

THUSNELDA   Dowager Duchess, may I speak?
Ladies. As I climbed up these creaking stairs
To bed, my candle suddenly was snuffed.
As I was near my bedroom, I held out
My hand to touch the door and find the handle.
I've done this many a draughty night. But no;
Feel as I would all up and down, no door
Was there. I groped along the smooth blank
    wall
Shivering with cold. Disoriented, lost,
I found my way down to your Highness' room
And gently knocked – but you were fast asleep.
I climbed the stairs again, now more confused
Until, as I was nightmared in despair,
A horse-like double laugh told me the Duke
And your Herr Goethe played a trick on me:
They had walled up my room!

AMALIA   *(Laughing)*   Now that's too bad
  Of them! They love their pranks – and you
    do,too,
Usually, my Thusnelda.

CHARLOTTE   I find it
Inconceivable Goethe and I
Should have become such strangers to each
    other.

LOTTE You needn't be. You say you can forgive.

CHARLOTTE My pain's not jealousy, or wounded pride
That he who fourteen years swore total love
To me holds her, who was a common whore,
Close as a poultice.

AMALIA   Then what makes you
   unhappy?

CHARLOTTE   Pain that a dear friend undermines himself,
            Squanders his high ideals, forgets his duty,
            And, like a cursed prince when dark midnight
                chimes
            Shrinks to a rat and scuttles to a sewer.

LOTTE   You healed me till I found illusion of death ...

CHARLOTTE   Became the death of illusion.

AMALIA   Harsh! Too hard!
            Humility means bearing humiliation –
            But all can still be well! Come, let's be merry!

THUSNELDA   *(Cheerfully)*   There's many an insult I have had
                to bury.

                    SCENE TWENTY

            HERDER *and* HÖLDERLIN.

HÖLDERLIN   Is my loneliness
            A blessing or a curse?

HERDER   It helps you write:
            And you have stared in Paris at the spoil
            Brought by Napoleon from Italy –
            Apollo Belvedere, Laocoön,
            The Capitoline Venus ...

HÖLDERLIN   Ah! Seeing them
            Broadened my understanding of all art.

HERDER   From Greece we take our standards, though
                the fall
            From that time to our own bruises the mind.

HÖLDERLIN   Longing creates. Athens inspires us till
            Her olive bears fruit on our German soil,

Our youth look to Olympia to train
Their bodies, while our womenfolk recall
Delos and Delphi till all nationhood
And politics flow with integrity
Shaped by religious awe's gift, lasting peace.

HERDER   A league of nations; not just present ones
But all who have loved good through history
Make up the league, and, to remotest time
Foreseen by Delphic utterance, the soul
Of every nation finds itself in verse.
Why, you have trudged the snow-majestic Alps
And turned them into half-mad poetry.

HÖLDERLIN   Where bright rock-cliffs of steep Parnassus
rise
Mounting to interfere where eagles turn
And wheel above the valley of the Pleistos
Which winds through olive trees of Cirrha's
plain
On to the sun-reflecting gulf of Corinth –
Delphi, first known as Pytho, chosen home
Of Zeus's radiant son, whose Pythoness
On sacred tripod utters oracles
Breathed through her by Apollo, neither
conceals
Nor states: just indicates. The healing god
Of harmony advises, not foretells.

HERDER   And I must indicate some tragic news ...

HÖLDERLIN   No! Not yet! Read a poem I have written.
Apollo has smitten me to recreate
From the sad wreck of lovers forced apart,
Who feel life withering, ebbing, slowly dying,
A wild imaginative lover's prayer
To art-immortal Echo!

HÖLDERLIN *hands* HERDER *a copy of his poem. They
read it aloud.*

HÖLDERLIN	Grant me, dear Echo, you who make many sing,
HERDER	*Echo:* Anything.
HÖLDERLIN	Susette creep in my bed of her free will.
HERDER	*Echo:* She will.
HÖLDERLIN	Our opportunity is never there!
HERDER	*Echo:* Sir, dare!
HÖLDERLIN	Tell how I love, whisper she come to me,
HERDER	*Echo:* Succumb to plea,
HÖLDERLIN	And I'll pay gold, plucked soft from her – one tress,
HERDER	*Echo:* Undress.
HÖLDERLIN	If you entice her naked through these doors.
HERDER	*Echo:* She's yours.

HERDER   You know your Greek Anthology, but those
Poems of comfort in adversity
Must be your consolation. Protesilaus
Returned from the cold kingdom of the
        shades
Because of his wife's, Laodamia's, prayers;
But she could not survive that anguished
        triumph.
Be careful how you call her, Hölderlin.
Susette is dead.

HÖLDERLIN   Diotima destroyed?

HERDER   She nursed her children through their
        German measles
And, her heart broken, weakly became
        infected.

HÖLDERLIN   The bright sun of her spirit is eclipsed,
And all that lovelier world we two had
        shared

On the volcano's edge in snow and fire
Is dark. Spread, scatter flowers, yield ripening
    fruit,
Oh God of love, soothe with eternal youth
And joy the woman I shall see no more.

SCENE TWENTY-ONE

GOETHE*'s house. Stage right:* GOETHE *in a cushioned
chair,* CHRISTIANA *with him.*

Enter SCHILLER *and* LOTTE.

SCHILLER   I've left my bed because I could not bear
Our lack of conversation any longer –
Another day going by not seeing your face.

GOETHE   Schiller, Schiller ...

GOETHE *and* SCHILLER *embrace.*

CHRISTIANA   For the last three months
The Privy-Councillor has scarcely had
One day of pain-free health.

LOTTE   So, too, my
    husband.

CHRISTIANA   He has a premonition either he
Or Schiller will die this year.

LOTTE   Yes, I know.

GOETHE   I work on notes to my translation of
Diderot's *Rameau's Nephew*; then dictate
My research: *History of Colour Theories.* You?

SCHILLER   Translated Racine's *Phèdre.*

GOETHE   It went down well
                    At the Court Theatre?

SCHILLER   No, it did not.
                    French Alexandrines swamp German blank
                        verse.

                    Fade.

                              SCENE TWENTY-TWO

                    SCHILLER*'s house. Stage left: the front door, out of
                    which comes* LOTTE, GOETHE *waiting.*

LOTTE   He's putting on his scarf. He will be thrilled
                    To see you here again after so long!

GOETHE   Lotte; is he well enough to go out?

LOTTE   I wonder.

                    Enter SCHILLER.

SCHILLER   My friend! You've recovered, come to visit me
                    Again! Come to the theatre!

GOETHE   What's on?

SCHILLER   One of those many plays spawned by your *Götz
                    Von Berlichingen* all those years ago.
                    You know, Ritterschauspiele: feudal knights
                    And chivalry: *Clara von Hoheneichen*
                    By that unemptying ink pot Christian Spiess.
                    Please come with us.

GOETHE   A slight indisposition
                    Prevents me joining you.

SCHILLER   They say your screams
Were heard by watchmen on the city gate.
I wept when I was told.

GOETHE   Every four weeks
A colic of my kidney cramps. Enough
Of me. You are far better!

SCHILLER   It's most strange:
The pain I've felt for years in my left lung
Has gone! *(Gasps for breath)* But Goethe, I am
       sad –
Although he used to preach in boots and
       spurs –
That Herder 's dead.

GOETHE   I never went to him
Without delighting in his tenderness;
Never left but sad at his bitterness.
Enjoy the play! Forgive me. Wiedersehen!

LOTTE AND ⎫
SCHILLER ⎬ Auf Wiedersehen!
          ⎭

SCENE TWENTY-THREE

SCHILLER *'s house. Stage left:* SCHILLER *in bed,
lighted candle by him.* ANNA AMALIA *and* LOTTE.

LOTTE   He came home feverish, with chattering teeth:
Scarcely caressed the children; seemed unclear
And incoherent. This is his champagne.

AMALIA   He asks for naphtha.

SCHILLER   Please – a pen and paper!

*'Lacrimosa' from Mozart's 'Requiem' begins, softly,
and continues until it is completed at the end of Act
One.* ANNA AMALIA *finds paper and pen and helps*
SCHILLER*'s attempt to write (unsuccessful), while*
LOTTE *goes into the next room and brings in their
nine-month old daughter,* EMILIE. SCHILLER *raises
himself up to look at her.*

LOTTE   Your daughter Emilie, my love! *(To* EMILIE*)* Your
               Daddy.

SCHILLER, *inarticulate, groans and turns over to
press his face in his pillow.* LOTTE *takes* EMILIE *out,
and returns as* SCHILLER *suddenly raises himself up
and in a loud, clear voice, looking up to the ceiling,
cries:*

SCHILLER   Sanctus fortis, Sanctus Deus,
                     De profundis oro te
                  Miserere Judex meus
                     Mortis in discrimine!

SCHILLER *dies on the eighth bar of the 'Lacrimosa',*
LOTTE *kneeling beside him wringing and kissing his
hands.* ANNA AMALIA *gently kisses his forehead and
then begins to leave: returns quietly to extinguish the
candle, then leaves* LOTTE *alone with her dead
husband. In the dark the 'Lacrimosa' plays.*

SCENE TWENTY-FOUR

GOETHE*'s house. Stage right:* GOETHE, *solus, in
cushioned chair with blanket.*

Enter CHRISTIANA.

GOETHE   Where has everyone gone?
               Voss left the house without saying 'Good-bye!'

Someone knocked, and then the front door
    banged.
Christiana, why are people avoiding
Me? Is something wrong? Is it the war?
Napoleon will fight the combined strength
Of both the Austrian and Russian armies
At Austerlitz. He cannot win! Though if ...
What would become of Weimar? Christiana,
Tell me the truth. Is Schiller very ill?
Fate is pitiless, and mankind small
Before it. Is he worse? Why do you cry?
Christiana. Is Schiller dead?

CHRISTIANA   He is.
He prayed aloud in Latin at the end.

GOETHE   Half my existence now is gone from me.
              (Though ill, GOETHE *throws off blanket and stands
              to his full height)*
              Go forth upon your journey, dear-loved soul,
              Go from this world!
              Go in the name of all that you have loved;
              Go in the name of all that we have shared;
              And may your dwelling place today, in peace,
              Be on the holy mount of Zion!

              GOETHE, *standing, raises his arms facing and
              leaning against a pillar and, with his back to the
              audience, sinks his face into his arms and silently
              weeps.*

              Mozart's 'Lacrimosa' finishes as lights fade to black.

              END OF ACT ONE

Act Two

GOETHE *'s house.*
GOETHE. *Enter to him, agitated,* CHRISTIANA.

CHRISTIANA   Emperor Napoleon is at the Castle Palace!

GOETHE   Karl August is not there. I warned the Duke
Not to join the defeated Prussians now
And take up his command in honoured
    madness!
Prince Hohenlohe-Inglefingen fled!

CHRISTIANA   Luise, the Duchess, who has been so kind
To me – has seemed to understand us two –
Stood at the top of the Palace stairs, alone:
Ministers, guards, all gone; just empty echo;
And faced the war-stained, sleepless, angry
    demon's
Climb unflinching. 'Look at that fearless
    woman!'
He said to General Rapp. 'What breeding!
    Worth
Two hundred cannon!'

GOETHE   But is the Duchess safe?

CHRISTIANA   With quiet dignity she pleaded for us;
Begged that the sack of Weimar should be
    stopped;
The burning houses, in whose flickering light
They faced each other, should be quenched
    and saved,
And pillage cease: the soldiers had enough.

GOETHE   What did Napoleon answer?

CHRISTIANA   'If within
                    Three days Karl August leaves the Prussian
                        army,
                    Withdraws his soldiers, and returns to Weimar,
                    I might not with my pencil cleanse the map
                    Of this state Saxe-Weimar; as I've done
                    With neighbouring Brunswick.'

GOETHE   Anna Amalia's home
                    Wiped off the map? What power is in that pen!

CHRISTIANA   If Karl August comes home he may still keep
                    All his dominions.

GOETHE   What a wife! What a
                    Duchess!

CHRISTIANA   Napoleon's anger flared up at the Duke's
                    Absence; jeered he'd been saved by a woman
                    Who took his place when cataclysm came.

GOETHE   Our Duke is helping wounded officers
                    And men robbed of their pay, trying to do
                    The impossible with a defeated army!
                    What would Napoleon do? Not be so generous
                    As our Karl August, lending lion-hearted
                        Blücher
                    Four thousand dollars after the battle of
                        Lübeck.
                    If our Duke's dispossessed, as in the past
                    His ancestor Duke John was, then I shall,
                    Like mine, old Lukas Cranach, follow him
                    My staff in hand through all the villages
                    While children point and say: 'There goes old
                        Goethe
                    The poet, with his one-time Duke of Weimar
                    Whom the French Emperor hurled from his
                        throne
                    Because he went to help his dying uncle,
                    And would not let defeated comrades starve!'

In every school they'll sing my songs of shame
Until they sing him on his throne again.

CHRISTIANA   My love, you go to bed. I'll clear away.
We must be ready for a dangerous day.
(*Exit* GOETHE)

SCENE TWO

CHRISTIANA *sola. Heavy knocks at the door. Sound of cannon shots.*

CHRISTIANA   Who's there?

1ST TIRAILLEUR   Two friends!

CHRISTIANA   Why the French
accents, then?

2ND TIRAILLEUR Open, or we will smash your windows.

CHRISTIANA *opens the door for them.*

CHRISTIANA   Come in.
Would you care for a glass of wine? We know
The Marshal Augereau's been billeted
With us; so you may see him.

1ST TIRAILLEUR   Coming here?
(CHRISTIANA *nods*) We thought we saw some
Prussians in your garden –
But it's so dark.

CHRISTIANA   We've many refugees.
Our garden's theirs in this catastrophe.

2ND TIRAILLEUR Another glass. (*The* TIRAILLEURS *drink*)

1ST TIRAILLEUR   Where is Goethe, then?

You are his 'sexy piece', 'eroticon'?
Eh? Eh? Where is he? Worn him out? Come
            here.

CHRISTIANA   He is upstairs, asleep.

2ND TIRAILLEUR   We'll get him up!
Yes, won't we! We'll be needing a dry bed!
More wine! Come on, let's find him!

TIRAILLEURS *go upstairs. Sounds of scuffle.*

CHRISTIANA   *(Calling out of the back window)* Some one help me!
Please! Some men. Two Frenchmen attack
            Goethe!
Go up the back stairs from the garden. Quickly!

Sounds of warm response from the garden.
Sounds of the TIRAILLEURS *being thrown out.*

Enter GOETHE, *unharmed, in his dressing gown.*

GOETHE   My love, you saved me by your strength of
            mind,
Wit, and unflinching fearlessness. I'll never
Hear any sneer at you again like that.
Please will you marry me?

CHRISTIANA   *(Taken aback)* Dearest, of course!

GOETHE   If we are still alive on Sunday next,
I'll ask our Christof Günther marry us
In the Court sacristy – his jurisdiction –
Quietly; with only Riemer and our son.
You are my Duchess, and my darling one.

Fade.

SCENE THREE

ANNA AMALIA, GOETHE *and* CHRISTIANA.

Wedding Music.

CHRISTIANA   Anna! Your Majesty!

AMALIA   My dear, a kiss.
I've come to bless your happiness. This war
Shadows the sunlight of your resolution
Like Rembrandt's brushstrokes. Blessings on
    your match!
My son delights in it as much as I.

CHRISTIANA   The Duke? And Duchess? Thank you, your
    Majesty,
You always smiled on us, trusted our love
When others raised their chins and spat.

AMALIA   Your ring:
Please may I feel it?

GOETHE   You see it's engraved
The fourteenth of October.

CHRISTIANA   *(Excitedly)*   Battle of Jena!

GOETHE   That was the bloody birth of my new epoch –
Different from your son's courting of Luise:
Those youthful preparations for his wedding
When he and I strolled round the streets of
    Paris.

AMALIA   Ah! You know all! As he was seventeen
His tutor Count Görtz had to guide my boy
Through necessary marriage preparations.
A small, discreet French woman called Jeanette
Brossard, of Epernay, taught him technique;

                And, in return, the grateful Weimar State
                Pays her a healthy pension to this day.

GOETHE   As our son's nearly seventeen, and I
                Am fifty-seven, it's possible I may
                Not need tender instruction from Jeanette.

AMALIA   Five hundred francs a year we're in her debt.
                Our Christiana – Mrs. Goethe now,
                And rightly so – look out across the park.
                October's touched the trees, and brown leaves
                    are
                Nature's grey hairs. My autumn slows my pace,
                But when I leave remember this embrace.

                AMALIA *silently embraces each, and leaves.*

                            SCENE FOUR

                A Ball.

                KLEIST, WILHELMINE *and* LUISE VON ZENGE.

KLEIST   Please may I have the honour of a dance?
                I am a nettle in your bed of flowers
                I know, a gaping mouth that eats up hopes,
                A headache you'd reverse Earth's axis to
                Be free from, but the crotchets of my fate
                Quaver you two tonight in these shared bars
                To harmonize discordant memories.

LUISE   Heine Kleist!

KLEIST   Would Wilhelmine glance
                Ever again in my direction?

LUISE   Yes,
                Of course, dear Heine! We are just the same –

Except she's married to Professor Krug,
Immanuel Kant's successor, and they're happy.
I'll introduce you to him ...

KLEIST
                              Dear Luise,
Golden as goodness, still; perhaps not yet.
I'm as unsure as a new foal's first step.

LUISE
Well, let me bring my sister Wilhelmine
Over. She will not wither you, or spit
Her tears to cloud strange opportunity.
She waited for you, and, while very ill,
She'd ask our little sister Emilie:
'Where is Kleist?'. The little toddler stood
Tip-toe each time and kissed your locket
      picture
Hanging beside her bed, or round her neck.
She's seen us. (WILHELMINE *comes over*)
(*To* WILHELMINE) He seems calmer and more
      serious.

WILHELMINE
Can past be the historic present? Ah!
You taught me much, dear Kleist. The giddy
      reach
Of your morality's swaying ideals
Left me with vertigo. Sublime instrument,
You were, by which our kind Creator God
Wished to ennoble me.

KLEIST
                        Oh, Wilhelmine,
I never seize the moment. Some strange flaw
Deep in my nature forces me to live
Either in past or future; settle down
Always where I am not. Forgive, forgive me!
Here's your tobacco pouch, which always
      hangs
From my vest's button. Yes, these are your
      gloves,
And your blue ribbon ...

WILHELMINE   I am married, Kleist.
              Please don't return to damn us. I'm content
                 now.

KLEIST   Man's first concern is not eternity
              But how he lives his earthly life. My fear
              Is not of hell but my own conscience. When
              In the grey dawn I rode away, I saw
              A figure move in the window. Passionately
              I longed to see if it were you. The coach
              Rolled on, my body twisted round, the house
              Pulled tears up through my eyes. Night,
                 parting, wept
              Soft, sprinkled drops. Over my head I pulled
              My coat, saw in that dark your eyes, your
                 breasts'
              Gold cross, your form, the movement of your
                 lips,
              The brown mark on the soft skin of your arm,
              And pressed my rainy sleeve in soaked
                 embrace.

LUISE   Dear friend, you had your chance – but did not
                 write!
              Or if you did, asked her to wait ten years.

KLEIST   Six, at the most.

LUISE   Demanded she become
              A peasant in Swiss costume on an island,
              While you worked in the fields.

KLEIST   That damned Consul
              Put paid to that! Oh my tormented heart
              Breeds me nothing but pain!

WILHELMINE   Come to our house
              And meet my husband. He knows all about
                 you.
              Tell us what you are writing.

KLEIST
A play in which
I ask if, when your husband loves you, you
Believe him to be me, he benefits,
Or you, or both? A story of a duel
In which the maid substitutes herself for
Her lady in the bed, and Redbeard takes
The lady's ring from her, not realizing.
Who is deceived? Who benefits?

WILHELMINE
Not now ...

KLEIST
Goethe is to perform my comedy ...

LUISE
Another time. Were you a Berlin student?

KLEIST
Every professor in his special field
Sat like a caterpillar on its leaf
Each thinking his one leaf was the whole tree ...

LUISE
I think you said the next dance was with me?

Dissolve into the Ball.

SCENE FIVE

HÖLDERLIN, FIRST MALE NURSE, *and* SECOND MALE
NURSE.

1ST NURSE
Where is the madman Hölderlin? Beard, teeth –
Tobacco-stained!

2ND NURSE
Watch out for those long nails!

1ST NURSE
They say he bangs the piano hours on end.

2ND NURSE
With nails like those?

1ST NURSE
He's strong: broad-
shouldered. Careful!

HÖLDERLIN	I do not want to be a Jacobin!
2ND NURSE	Let's listen what he says.
HÖLDERLIN	Long live the King!
1ST NURSE	The horses ready? He may struggle.
2ND NURSE	Yes; And try to throw himself out of the coach.
HÖLDERLIN	Mock not the child who spurs his wooden horse, And with his whip fancies him brave and great. Oh, loved Germans, we too are weak In actions, rich in dreams.
2ND NURSE	Sounds disloyal.
HÖLDERLIN	Yet even today the light above still calls! With devout songs I shall propitiate You, holy shades, Until my soul grows wholly used To living with you ...
1ST NURSE	You must live with us, sir. Greetings! Yes.
HÖLDERLIN	Are you armed men coming to kidnap me?
1ST NURSE	Armed, poet? No! We've come to keep you safe. Your mother says you're dangerous to the public; And, what is more, the public may stone you If, in their irritation, they come near.
2ND NURSE	Is it your piano-playing?
HÖLDERLIN	Where will you take me?
1ST NURSE	To Dr. Authenrieth's fine clinic at Tübingen University.

HÖLDERLIN   With students?

2ND NURSE   Yes.
You'll be paraded as a specimen.
You see this mask? Ferdinand Authenrieth
Invented it to stop his patients screaming.
All you need do is breathe in.

1ST NURSE   Ah! Well done!

2ND NURSE   Don't fight your friends!

1ST NURSE   If you're inquisitive,
I'm told you may have yet three years to live.
(HÖLDERLIN *is bundled out*)

SCENE SIX

WIELAND, GOETHE *and* CHARLOTTE VON STEIN.

WIELAND   My friend, I've read your new play in the verse
Anthology they publish every year.
Your play's well-named *Pandora*! I see it
As covert comment on the evils now
Unleashed by this titanic Buonaparte
Whose high, triumphal entry through Berlin
In bloody conquest is theatrical
As is the raft, with tent and twin armchairs,
Moored midstream in the river Niemen by
French engineers; with flags, mirrors, table
At which Tsar Alexander signs away
All Russian armies from opposing France.
The Emperors of East and of the West
Are each rowed out. The river holds its breath
As drums roll, and the silver trumpets climb
Above the gun-salutes as both embrace,
Row back, to leave the demon free to reap
His harvest of all Europe. Prussia? Gone.
The Holy Roman Empire? Killed and buried.

GOETHE   And now, on top of this, Amalia's died.

WIELAND   We owe all that we have to her. Wing words
                To be read out from every pulpit in
                The country, consecrating memory!
                She brought me here as tutor to her son
                Karl August, to prepare his mind for rule.
                And he, the Duke, brought you; and you
                    brought Herder ...

GOETHE   Who for a while stole your friendship from me.

WIELAND   Never, dear Goethe!

GOETHE   Anna made Weimar
                A garden of the Muses where we strayed
                And stayed. She loved all laughter, wrote the
                    music
                For my Singspiel, *Erwin and Elmire*
                So well, made it so popular, it has
                Been played most often of my theatre-works.

                Enter CHARLOTTE VON STEIN.

CHARLOTTE   My tribute, may I add?

GOETHE   Charlotte, please do!

CHARLOTTE   Her Friday evenings once a month brought all
                Of us together in her house. We read
                Aloud your works, both of you; Shakespeare's
                    too;
                And Lessing's. When there was a gala ball
                The Court would come at eight, and she would
                    dress
                As a Greek Queen, or – at another time –
                Dazzle with flashing gems, her Princes dressed
                As Zephyr and Amour. Her dancing was
                Graceful, and lightly stepped, untiring, free
                To every masked man who invited her;

And over at the faro table where
The lowest stake was half a gulden, she
Would generously stake dollars, half-louis
And play and dance till three o'clock!

WIELAND   What days!
She loved to mix with students after dusk,
Join in their rude songs as they walked her
        home
Through Belvedere's garden nightingales.

GOETHE   And she became my mother's loyal friend,
Visited her, and wrote continual letters.
She painted, and gave us our theatre ...

CHARLOTTE   Above all, gave us peace as best she could,
And was creative in her widowhood.

GOETHE   She wore her titles lightly; with respect
As was appropriate – always to protect.

CHARLOTTE   As Regent of this little State she steered
Through debt, divisions, jealousies and claims,
To make our cultured Weimar loved, not feared.
Her golden memory no one defames.

SCENE SEVEN

Garden of GOETHE *'s Garden House.*

GOETHE *and* CHRISTIANA.

GOETHE   Here, crush these heart-shaped leaves. This
        one's called Balm.
Now raise it to your face.

CHRISTIANA   It smells of lemons!

GOETHE   We'll plant midwinter honeysuckle leaves

Below and round this slope, so promised
    fragrance
Lightens short days and smiles through early
    dusk.
Then, stronger-scented herbs and meadow
    flowers
To beckon loitering Spring – yellow archangel,
Blood on its lips; the straggling pennyroyal,
Buttonweed, tansy, calamint, and wormwood ...

CHRISTIANA   May we plant lavender?

GOETHE   Along that path.
Now, coming closer down, more gentle stems:
Water-mint by this cascade, marjoram,
Soft-scented basil, wild and aspiring – try!
(She picks and smells some basil)
Large daisy chamomile (not her stinking sister),
The white, thyme-scented horehound (not the
    dark –
Too pungent). All around your favourite seat
We'll breathe the violet hyssop's gentle sighs
Mingled with bright blue meadow-clary's
    breeze
Until all lifts to airy harmony
And drifts to the far wallflowers' heavy scent.

CHRISTIANA   You love your garden; and this park of trees:
All nature.

GOETHE   Each of her works has unique
Integrity. All that she gives is good.
She has no past or future, rest, or language,
But creates hearts and tongues through which
    she feels.
Her every goal is Love. No one knows when
She'll suddenly abandon her sweet dance.
All she creates we recognize as new
And age-old. Infinite variety
Is one; changing eternally the same.

CHRISTIANA   Did you brood on these plants when you were
      ill,
    Those desperate days before we two had met?

GOETHE   I did, and studied other mysteries –
    The Cabbalistic secrets, cryptograms
    And sacred correspondences obscure ...

CHRISTIANA   And did it help to heal?

GOETHE   Yes, insofar
    As my long-incubating *Faust* drew strength
    From some such studies as the alchemists ...

CHRISTIANA   If only you would finish this strange work,
    So unlike that white building you inspired
    Across the meadow: the Duke's Roman House
    With four – 'ionic' pillars, do you call them?

GOETHE   My *Faust* is from my darker, childhood world
    Of puppet plays, of shrunk, long-withered
        heads
    On iron spikes at Frankfurt's city gates.
    When I was twenty-two, and a young lawyer,
    A serving-maid from a near Frankfurt inn,
    Susanna Margaretha Brandt, in fear
    Killed her new babe. The Devil had seduced her,
    She said, a travelling goldsmith using drugs.
    Her prison was in smelling distance of
    My home. Our Doctor Metz examined her.
    As she was carried through cold winter streets
    The church bell tolled. Above her a white rod
    Was snapped in token of damnation as
    They bound her to Hell's chair. The sword was
        large,
    And as the executioner was old
    And felt he may not have the weight or
        strength
    To behead with one blow, he called his son
    Whom the hushed crowd saw roll it at a stroke.

CHRISTIANA   Decapitated for infanticide!

GOETHE   I had myself loved ten months, then
         abandoned
Friederike Brion, just before.
Wife, can you see why Faust and Gretchen writhe
Still in my thoughts? Friederike was young,
Eighteen. She never married; never healed.

CHRISTIANA   My husband, no more thoughts like these.
         Come in.
There is a packet for you ...

GOETHE   Yes, I know.
Lord Peter von Haza ...

CHRISTIANA   With the pouting wife?

GOETHE   Sophie is beautiful, and has four children!
Lord Peter's sent me Adam Müller's script
To write some comments on. As Müller 's close friend
Of Kleist, whose play we're acting, I must read,
Encourage, carefully; sort flower from weed.
(Exeunt)

SCENE EIGHT

ADAM MÜLLER *and* KLEIST.

KLEIST   Adam Müller, you whom August Schlegel
Called 'a divine man of unfathomed learning',
You for whom all the Catholic writers come
To Lord von Haza's soirées ...

MÜLLER   Lady von Haza's.

KLEIST   You, tutor to his children, are not sacked?

MÜLLER   Kleist, our immortal genius, yes; I am –
     Well, by agreement. My friend, I'm in love ...

KLEIST   Oh not with his wife, with the thirty-two-
     Year-old Sophie von Haza's busty charms!

MÜLLER   She's had four children – what do you expect?

KLEIST   To make love to her.

MÜLLER   You?

KLEIST   Yes, I myself:
     I've got to have her. If you're in my way
     I'll toss you from the next bridge in the river.

MÜLLER   My dear friend, I am serious. She loves me.
     For God's sake don't let's quarrel. Lord von
           Haza
     Knows of our love-making. They will divorce,
     And I shall marry her.

KLEIST   And feed the children?
     Adam Müller, if I find my place
     Nowhere on earth, perhaps a better one
     Waits me on some far star. You deftly prove
     Why I'm heartsick of all society.
     A sad truth: bluntly, I do not like people.

MÜLLER   Women?

KLEIST   Their prudish, feigned hypocrisy
     Recoils as from a snake inside a pillow
     At my attempts in plays and prose to show
     The truth of love. When in an audience
     They falsify their feelings, and the play!

MÜLLER   Your *Penthesilea*, your *Marquise of O*,
     Magnificent in manner, art and style,
     Cannot be – as my writings can – dismissed

Because they disturb. Each is moral, true,
And, like the sea, engrossing, flowing back
Into the far shores of our consciousness
Long after they are seen no more. Such work –
It's the past's wisdom and experience
Of most great books – may have to circulate
Around the Earth for thirty years or more,
Orphaned, before one mind appreciates
It fully, and unveils it to the world.

KLEIST   Look, I can't wait that long!

MÜLLER   No, nor can I.
Goethe has read, and 'studied with mixed
          feelings'
My work *On German Literature and Science.*

KLEIST   Well, Friedrich Schlegel liked it.

MÜLLER   What did Goethe
Say of impassioned *Penthesilea?*

KLEIST   'Unplayable', he wrote. 'In certain places
The tragedy verges on comedy.'

MÜLLER   And did the Olympian condescend some
            more?

KLEIST   'I'll have to come to know her. As it is
She comes from a too wondrous race for me ...'
As if my foaming-jawed hyena, she-wolf,
Were evening-gowned at Sophie Haza's soirée!
I'm waiting now to hear how my new play
Goethe's produced, *The Broken Water-Pitcher*,
Has been received.

MÜLLER   Haven't you heard? Why I ...

SCENE NINE

LORD PETER VON HAZA, *his young son*, ADAM MÜLLER
and KLEIST.

Enter HAZA *and* SON.

HAZA   Adam Müller, may I speak with you?

MÜLLER   Come in! Lord Peter von Haza, this is Kleist.
            Kleist, stay! My Lord von Haza ...

HAZA   I am here
            To thank you for your care of my young son
            And all that you have taught him.

MÜLLER   Yes, we are
            Good friends; I hope for ever.

HAZA   But you plucked
            The apple when employed to water seeds.

MÜLLER   I'm sorry, sir. On your estate at Posen,
            (*Crouching down to conjure up the scene for the boy*)
            If you go out at dawn, when drifting mist
            Covers the forest hills and swirls to hide
            The intermittent, glancing sun, your herd
            Of deer flick their ears at high speed, more
                like
            Butterflies. They eat twitching, like a rabbit,
            Wagging their tails. Why, from behind they
                look
            Just like a parliament of badgers! Soft!
            When one stands upright, and its graceful neck
            Is lifted high, the ears and eyes alert
            A moment, scenting peace yet not quite sure,
            Then turns its head right round to lick a
                haunch;
            Or a fawn shoves its wet nose in white fur

Of the hind's underbelly for warm milk –
Spread, frozen cobwebs glistening blades of
    grass –
One has a pulse-stopped wonder at such grace,
Such passionate longing to applaud such beauty,
You might as well attempt to hide the wind
As lock appreciation in your heart.

HAZA   The stag, though set apart, yet still combines
Majesty with an extreme tenderness.
Please may our clever hunter leave, and take
His net with him? Melt, let the herd remain?
The hind is needed by her little ones;
And who can tell what anguish antlers hide?

MÜLLER   Your graceful Sophie's love for you has died.
(*Exit* HAZA)

SCENE TEN

ADAM MÜLLER *and* KLEIST.

KLEIST   There is a smell of rotting apples here.
Your self-assurance could be misconstrued
As bland self-righteousness.

MÜLLER   I champion
Your *Penthesilea* play when all my friends
Sneer that friendship distorts my true
    judgement.

KLEIST   Oh, it's like that, is it, Adam? By God,
I merely made the verses not the world!
The play reflects that as it is. Are we
To bring to life our *Journal for the Arts*
Together, to unite this country's best
Writers and thinkers, while you separate
Your charges from their mother, wreck their
    lives?

MÜLLER   You have not paid the capital you promised
To start our magazine. When will it come?

KLEIST   Don't change the subject.

MÜLLER   Right! *You* lust for her!

KLEIST   But what she might give me she still retains.
No one is hurt as no one knows our games.

MÜLLER   By God, you'll have none!

KLEIST   She's not Eve.

MÜLLER   Just
mine!
You asked how your play Goethe has produced
Went down? Ha! It was a catastrophe!
A hopeless failure! Stilted, dragged out, slack;
Talk on the stage, talk in the theatre stalls:
One lad was gaoled for whistling. They could
     not
Prison the entire audience. You are
Discredited by Goethe and the Court
And held in anger and contempt.

KLEIST   When you
Read out my work aloud, you know it sounds
Like nasal bellows leaking. You expect
Me to applaud your massacre of art?

MÜLLER   You begged, then praised my public readings.
     Choose
Your weapons. He who wins will take the wife.

KLEIST   Adam, you are not worth my wasted life.

Exeunt left and right.

SCENE ELEVEN

GOETHE. *Enter to him* KLEIST.

GOETHE   Come in, Heine; if you are not already!

KLEIST   Zeus, you have hurled your thunderbolt at me!

GOETHE   Whatever do you mean?

KLEIST   You massacred
          My comic masterpiece!

GOETHE   No; that's not true.
          I took more time and trouble than I should
          To groom your slow and static play about
          A trial into something that could work.

KLEIST   You broke it into three acts, wrecked the flow,
          Tension, and atmosphere with intervals!
          Where is the menace if you stop for drinks?
          Who can enjoy a comic tale in chunks?

GOETHE   Let me tell you what happened.

KLEIST   Oh, I know.
          I've read the gloating, supercilious
          Journal for the Fashionable World
          Review, suggesting it become one act.
          That's what it is! One act of thirteen scenes!

GOETHE   They mean compressed. It's too long for no
               action.
          They felt the malice in your comedy.

KLEIST   I'm glad they laughed!

GOETHE   They didn't. I went out
          Myself to hush that restless audience,

And said: 'Each of you who disrupts this work's
First showing ought to be ashamed! Behave!'
By Act Two it was worse. Duke Karl August
Leaned over to shout down to his Hussars
To arrest a shrill whistler. By Act Three
The stamping feet, the coughing, and the talk
So drowned the actors they could not be heard.
They mouthed your text until the curtain fell.

KLEIST   Your central actor was incompetent
To play the part of Adam.

GOETHE   He was weak;
But I worked hard on him.

KLEIST   He endlessly
Screwed up his face and drawled; was far too slow
I'm told. You only took, produced, my play
In order to encourage me.

GOETHE   The world,
Dear Kleist, is a cracked bell at best. I hoped
We might reveal your gifts; is that so wrong?
Your leaf blown by the wind looked like a bird.

KLEIST   With your faint praise, your butchery of my text,
Actors incompetent, feeble direction,
You've not ignored, you have dishonoured me;
And I will tear the laurel from your head:
If not outclassing you in genius,
Then with two swords, or pistols. You may choose.

GOETHE   A challenge? I have loved, promoted, praised
You and your work. Defeat is just one step!
Send me your drama *Käthchen of Heilbronn*
To read. You've genius, humour, language, wit,
Now add swift-moving action. Please don't let
Morbidity destroy your universe.
A challenge to a friend 's surely perverse!

Fade.

SCENE TWELVE

KLEIST *and* HENRIETTE VOGEL *at the piano.*

KLEIST   Henriette Vogel, as you play
Your fingers draw up waves of the sea, and
          drown
All miseries that ever I have felt.

HENRIETTE   My darling love, my feather on the waves
Rolled to and fro, but light, and still afloat
To cup your stem into a tender boat
That gently lifts this ill and sinking friend;
(Indicating herself)
Let's leave the music hanging in the air.

KLEIST   Your playing is so beautiful I could
This moment shoot myself.
(Pause, as HENRIETTE *looks long at him)*
                                        We are so close
Shall we share secret intimacies?

HENRIETTE   How?

KLEIST   Let's tell each other our past love-affairs,
Stripped of all prudish reticence.

HENRIETTE   Do you
Want that? Well; if it pleases you, I will.
You know that I loved Adam Müller, and
When he left me for younger Sophie Sander ...

KLEIST   Wife of the fat, good, crazy publisher!
Well, Adam has another Sophie now.

HENRIETTE   Franz Theremin, Adam's friend, became my
          joy.

KLEIST   But *he* has Sophie Sander as *his* mistress!

HENRIETTE Yes. Each left me for her. She's twenty-three;
No pockmarks on her cheeks, and smaller
      breasts.
I'm ten years older.

KLEIST   You've a young eagle's soul!
I'm 'wearing Müller's cast-off bedroom
      slippers',
They say, who cannot recognize that you
Alone know that my sadness is sublime,
Incurable, deep-rooted. I have found
The glory of the human spirit matched
Only by you. I will do anything
You ask.

HENRIETTE *(Playfully)* So will my darling husband! *(Plays
      piano for a few bars)* I
Shall whisper to these green walls they keep
      hushed
A task that I may set. *(Plays a chord. Raises hand)*
      I won't be rushed.

SCENE THIRTEEN

CHRISTIANA, WIELAND. *Enter to them* GOETHE.

CHRISTIANA Where you grow up conditions you, and that
Decision 's made by your parents.

WIELAND   You were saved
By your own Privy-Councillor. My soul's
As full of Goethe as a dew-drop is
Filled with the morning's sun!

CHRISTIANA   Herr Doctor
      Wieland;
Did you have an illegitimate son
By a young Catholic girlfriend long ago?

WIELAND   In Biberach, yes: before I was married.
                  Clearly, no secret!

CHRISTIANA   That's why you understood
                  My husband and myself when most condemned;
                  As they did once more when we had our
                        wedding,
                  Which our son, August, witnessed for us with
                  My husband's secretary, Riemer.

WIELAND   Ah!
                  Even devoted, testy, Herder quipped
                  Of Goethe's play *The Natural Daughter*, 'I
                  Prefer your natural son!' – and hurt him
                        deeply.

CHRISTIANA   Poor Herder! Yet he generously said
                  'Your husband's absolutely free from any
                  Spirit of intrigue'.

WIELAND   And it's true!

                  Enter GOETHE.
                                            We are
                  Discussing the strange couplings of the sexes.

GOETHE   Do we have choice? To love on earth's to suffer.
                  I'm fascinated by the Swedish chemist
                  Torbern Bergman's 'attractio electiva'.
                  He isolates chemical elements
                  And studies their attraction and repulsion.
                  I've made a story of four characters –
                  Baron Eduard, and his wife Charlotte,
                  Who welcome to their friendship Ottilie –
                  A girl, and an efficient, tidy Captain.
                  Is it fate, chemical affinities,
                  That draw this square into two triangles?
                  As Charlotte clasps her husband and conceives
                  She feels the Captain in her arms, while he
                  Imagines in return young Ottilie.

No. They do not commit adultery –
With bodies; only minds. The baby born
Has the girl's eyes and Captain's body. It
Must die: that night must claim its monstrous
    debt.
How can they say I'm not a Christian?

WIELAND   Poor Hölderlin and Susette paid their price!

CHRISTIANA   But Adam Müller's married Sophie now!

GOETHE   No more! Don't probe for origins in life.
Everything in this book I've lived, but nothing
In it has not been changed. An open wound
Of passion is its source, which dreads to heal.

WIELAND   You chill me. Here is Kleist's *Käthchen of*
          Heilbronn
Returned: a play that takes up my own thoughts
On otherworldly guidances in our
Compulsion towards human happiness.

GOETHE   A common girl and a young nobleman
The same night dream the same dream! I will
    not
(GOETHE *flings the manuscript in the fire*)
Direct this grotesque fairy-tale, with its
Illegitimacy, intrigue, birthmarks,
Somnambulism, angels, water-sprites –
Not if half Weimar begs to see it!

CHRISTIANA   I
Like the strange story. Does the patient girl
Make the count love her? Do they marry?

WIELAND   Yes,
By heavenly powers protected; after trials.

GOETHE   The ending of Kleist's play *Amphitryon*
Is weak; the hero's fate is cruel, his wife's

Embarrassing. Here it's just sentimental
Wish-fulfilment. Something about Kleist –
Nordic, Prussian, acrimonious –
Is barbaric, mis-shapen; it revolts
As if what nature had intended to
Be beautiful were blasted with disease.
His angel forehead bears the mark of Cain.

WIELAND   That's ripe, from one who makes Faust live
         again!

Fade to black.

SCENE FOURTEEN

GOETHE*'s house.* CHRISTIANA *and* GOETHE.

CHRISTIANA   The Duke has summoned you to Erfurt.

GOETHE   Yes.
My mother has just died. She had the gift
Of happiness; and storytelling: both
Of which she gave me. She was seventy-seven.
My father gave me *gravitas*; his build.
A quarter century she outlived him!

CHRISTIANA   Your mother loved you wholly, to the end:
You were her glory and her happiness.

GOETHE   And she was mine – although I seldom saw her!
Come, what's the gossip?

CHRISTIANA   Don't be shy to mourn.
Tsar Alexander met Napoleon
Midway across the Niemen on a raft
To mark the Tilsit treaty. Now, halfway
Between Erfurt and Weimar they embrace
At Münchenholzen to drill, and prepare
Their entry into Erfurt side by side.

GOETHE   That French, demonic Emperor rules Europe!
           If one compares such nations to our own
           It is embarrassing. Science and art
           Are wings which raise us, but no substitute
           For the proud consciousness of being part
           Of a great nation, powerful and feared;
           Respected. Well; Napoleon may be right:
           'Not yet the destiny of Germany!'
           I do believe our future holds that promise.
           All we can do is, individually,
           Give all our talents, energies and thoughts
           To spreading a sound culture, up and down,
           Especially up – so leaders are humane;
           And intellectually we do not falter,
           But remain fresh, creative, strong, alert,
           Ready, and not found wanting, when that day
           Of glory dawns.

CHRISTIANA   Darling, you must go.
           You're needed. See Napoleon and the Tsar.
           Clap hands each night: Champagned, with
                caviar
           Slice the cake Europe at his escritoire!

                       SCENE FIFTEEN

           Erfurt. NAPOLEON *'s breakfast.*

           TALLEYRAND, NAPOLEON *and his* COURT. *Enter to
           them* GOETHE.

TALLEYRAND Monsieur Goethe, welcome to us! I'm
           Charles de Talleyrand. The Emperor
           Will see you now. He's eating breakfast. Ah!

NAPOLEON   Talleyrand! Berthier! Daru! Savaray!
           If I had been alive I would have made
           Corneille a prince. Where are the maps of

Poland?
Send in the poet Goet!

Enter GOETHE.

                         Voilà un homme!
Monsieur Goet: I'm very pleased to meet you.
How old are you?

GOETHE   Sixty, Emperor.

NAPOLEON   Vous êtes un homme. You're well-preserved.
              Married?

GOETHE   And with a boy of nineteen.

NAPOLEON   Ah! C'est bien!

GOETHE   I see that when your Majesty is travelling
              Even the smallest details are observed.

NAPOLEON   You are Germany's greatest tragic poet.

GOETHE   Poor country if I am. We have our share
              Of great men: Schiller, Wieland, Lessing.

NAPOLEON   Oui?
              I've read Schiller's *History of the Long War.*
              Tragedies drawn from that would, frankly, be
              Fitter for the Paris boulevards than us.

GOETHE   Your Majesty ...

NAPOLEON   Come to the theatre
              Tonight. The Théâtre Français will perform
              Racine's *Iphigénie.* It is good,
              Though not my favourite. There you will see
              On my parterre some golden crowns of
                   Europe.
              Have you yet met the Tsar?

GOETHE   Emperor, no;
                     Although I hope to be presented to him.

NAPOLEON   He speaks good German. Why don't you
                             describe
                     These history-shaping days, and dedicate
                     What you write to him – as the poets did
                     At Versailles for the King Louis Quatorze?

GOETHE   It's true they did, sire; but your Majesty
                     Does not know whether they repented it.
                     I have an old rule never to dedicate;
                     It keeps my conscience, and my options, clear.

NAPOLEON   How do you like our visit?

GOETHE   We are dazzled,
                     Hoping it brings a blessing on our country.

NAPOLEON   Are the Duke's subjects happy?

GOETHE   They have high hopes.

NAPOLEON   Monsieur Goet; ride with us on our tour.
                     Immortalize power imperial
                     Unfolded in magnificent display.
                     The glory would be yours.

GOETHE   Ah! Emperor:
                     I'd need the classic pen of ancient times
                     To do you justice.

NAPOLEON   Tacitus, you admire?

GOETHE   Deeply. Sire, I do.

NAPOLEON   Well, I do not:
                     That slanderer of the Caesars! Your Karl August
                     Has been behaving badly for some time;
                     But he's been punished for it.

GOETHE   If he has,
                 Sire, and I've no judgement in these things,
                 Then you are right: His punishment has been
                 Severe: but may I say the Duke protects
                 Learning, and all the arts? From us there is
                 Nothing but praise for him.

NAPOLEON   I've read your *Werther* seven times; took it to
                 The Sphinx. Why do you mix the motivation?
                 He kills himself for love, not failed ambition.
                 Mixing the two weakens the all-consuming
                 Passion of his desire. What says Herr Goet?

GOETHE   *(Smiling)* Your point is deft. I'm not sure it's
                      been made
                 Before. It was a way to end the book;
                 One can't leave it to Fate!

NAPOLEON   Fate! That great weakness of French theatre!
                 Why don't they look at nature, and stop
                      wailing.
                 Politics, policy is Fate!

                 Marshal DARU *enters with maps of Poland.*

GOETHE   *(Aside)* The old scene, with new players on the
                      stage.
                 Same wallpaper. Where have the portraits
                      gone?
                 That's where Anna Amalia used to hang
                 In a ball dress, holding a velvet mask.

NAPOLEON   *(To* DARU*)* The Poles are restless? Say I
                      promised them
                 Some independence, and they wait for it?
                 Show me that map. If we divide and rule ...
                 Think it through for a moment.
                 (Turning to GOETHE, *and taking him, privately,*
                      downstage)   Tragic plays
                 Should educate both subjects and their rulers

In suffering, its causes; in endurance.
There is no higher laurel crown than this
For a great poet. Write on Caesar's death –
Better than Voltaire did. Your masterpiece!
Show how had Caesar been allowed his scope,
Time to complete his vision, then the world
And history would bow to him, and bless.
Come to see Racine's *Andromaque* as well;
And here's my invitation: come to Paris:
My personal request. There you will find
Far wider truths to stimulate your mind –
Your genius for observation spurred
To inspiration mankind's never heard.

GOETHE   I am most grateful, sire. You honour me.

NAPOLEON   Now, Poland!

> GOETHE *stands aside, and gestures to* TALLEYRAND
> *to ask if he can leave.* TALLEYRAND *approaches*
> NAPOLEON *who, still studying the map, nods, but*
> *does not look up.* TALLEYRAND *indicates to* GOETHE
> *he may leave. Exit* GOETHE *and fade scene.*

SCENE SIXTEEN

The Ballroom at Weimar Castle. The Court Ball.
Music.

NAPOLEON, METTERNICH *attending in background.*
GOETHE, WIELAND, PRUSSIAN OFFICER.

NAPOLEON   No, I don't dance. Tell me, Monsieur Goet;
                Did you rebuild, design this masterpiece?

GOETHE   This pillared ballroom, white and gold? It was
                My concept, and built under my direction.
                The Berlin architect Herr Heinrich Gentz
                Designed these public rooms.

NAPOLEON   *(Looking round ballroom)* A double cube?
              You've brought classic perfection into being,
              And on a human scale, unlike Versailles.
              At my command we've toured the battlefield
              At Jena, and, to celebrate our visit –
              And remind all my army crushed the
                    Prussians –
              Chased a hare-hunt: that's how they ran from
                    us!
              (NAPOLEON *laughs,* GOETHE *and* WIELAND *do not*)
              Look! Here's your soldier who will tell you all.
              (NAPOLEON moves away)

PRUSSIAN   Have you stalked deer? The hare? They had
OFFICER   two hunts.
              The Duke had filled a groaning shooting-stand
              With half the royalty of Europe, while
              The Tsar, so blind he scarcely sees his breath,
              Had a great stag, wide and heavy of bone,
              Brought to bay just five paces from his nose.
              The Emperor of Russia managed to
              Transfix that antlered crown of tender fear
              Through the eye. Forty-six more stags were
                    killed
              For banqueting at six o'clock.

WIELAND   Fresh meat!
              But what about the hare?

PRUSSIAN   Ah yes, the hare.
OFFICER   Marvellous beast. The Prussian delegate,
              Prince Wilhelm, had been compelled to attend
              And see the tent in which the battlefield
              Was laid out with toy soldiers; but the hare,
              Weaving and turning, shaking off its scent
              Amongst this tent of boots, the cunning hare
              Leaped on the table twitching, paused to pant,
              Then turned alertly, scattering the toys.
              Napoleon roared with laughter, slapped the
                    Prince

Hard on his Prussian back and said: 'You ran
Like hares, and like this hare we smashed your
    plan!'

NAPOLEON *returns.*

Great and victorious Emperor from Paris!
I'm sorry for our hunt all that you had
Was my small woodman's cottage.

NAPOLEON   Fellow soldier –
Like me, since boyhood? Makes me feel at home!
The echoing Paris palaces bore me,
Soon make me restless. We, friend, are at ease
Only in pitched camp: woodsmoke, and the
    guns!
Only live fully on a battlefield.
(NAPOLEON *pats him on the shoulder – sends him
off, elated*)

METTERNICH   Silence, please! The Emperor of France
Wishes to speak.

NAPOLEON   Thank you. I thank Weimar
For all your lavish loyalty and welcome!
I see a banner in the street outside:
What do the words mean?

METTERNICH   Emperor, it says
'If now on earth still walked God's Son
His name would be Napoleon.'
(*Polite applause*)

NAPOLEON   Most satisfactory. Now here, to end
This day's commemoration of our visit,
(I'm pleased to see that obelisk outside:
Make it in stone soon) I shall see your poets
Goet, and Doctor Wieland – whom I find
Makes German language sound almost like
    French

In polished grace, sophisticated ease –
Each, on this memorable day, receive
From me the French Cross of the Légion
    d'Honneur.
(NAPOLEON *bestows the crosses to full-hearted*
applause)
One blessing more. Three hundred thousand
    francs
To help emergency rebuilding here
I'll send. I leave for Spain now to subdue
And free them. Your Duke's Weimar troops are
    spared
That active service this time! I am gone.

Hearty applause.

SCENE SEVENTEEN

NAPOLEON *and* METTERNICH.

METTERNICH   Sire, will you take this army? Some of them –
I've seen them – are no more than children;
    our
Anticipated generation.

NAPOLEON   *(Angry)* You
Are not a soldier. My whole life has been
The battlefield. A true professional
Like me does not blanch at a million lives
Lost in war!

METTERNICH   Shall I open the door
So all of France and Germany can hear
Your words?

NAPOLEON   Prince Metternich, I have
Protected France! Most of the lives are
    Prussian.

METTERNICH   And you are speaking to a German, Sire.
              If you think this way, Emperor, you are lost.
              (NAPOLEON *spits on the floor and turns away*)

              Exeunt opposite ways.

                        SCENE EIGHTEEN

                 GOETHE *and* WIELAND.

WIELAND   What do you make of our new Emperor?
              The demon?

GOETHE   Like Raphael, or Mozart; Shakespeare:
              Perfect at what they do. They tower above
              Mankind, are unattainable. He is
              Always enlightened, clear-headed; a match
              For every challenge: day or night he has
              Mental energy, full strength to confront
              And master each. Strides like a demi-god
              From victory to battle victory!
              A dull, prosaic city like Berlin
              Could never spark such a world-conqueror,
              Nor would it have occassion to. His youth
              Is self-renewing, and his destiny
              More brilliant than the world has ever seen
              Or will see after him; dwarfs other kings,
              Popes, Emperors – a born ruler of the world.
              I can't forgive him wounding German pride
              Deliberately with hare hunts; the cost
              Of this extravagant festivity
              When half our town's been plundered by his
                        troops;
              But, with his white-hot will and serene aim,
              Europe will never see his like again.

PRUSSIAN   *(Passing by again and overhearing)*
OFFICER   All I can say is, I would gladly shed

My blood to be rid of him and his French:
We hate the murderous foreigner! Good-bye!

SCENE NINETEEN

KLEIST, *solus, writing.*

As KLEIST *speaks he rises, leaving his writing, and
with a single spotlight on him in the dark, addresses
the audience.*

KLEIST   Breathe me my voice through sky-resounding
                        brass
From the gold-cloud-touched, terrifying peak
Of highest, snow-dragged Herz, that it may
                        ring
To harangue Prussia, Austria, the whole
Divided German nation to unite
Against our tyrant-master-enemy.
Our leaders fear our peoples' army? Shame!
Strangle your vested interests, and dread
Of rebels; your old weakness, rivalry.
Fail to be flattered by French courtesy
Whose magnanimity culls gratitude
Their friendly, generous, calm, ennobling
                        banks
Afford through unimaginable spoils of war.
Be single-minded for the sacred fire
Of freedom! Every thought subordinate
To our loved land; yes, even moral scruple –
For morals win no wars. Exult to hurl
Our slavery under the foreign fist
Into the reeling past! You German wife
Blue-eyed and blonde-haired, tease their
                        fighting boys
Into your warm pit, one by one; then watch
In glee un-horrified as a she-bear
Rips off young limbs mauling in famished fur.

Drink no milk of forgiveness – rape such
    thought!
Fathers of girls thrust by French soldiers, kill
Your daughters, then dismember them and
    send
A portion to each German tribe to spur
Its fighting wrath! If any man has courage,
Fanaticism, cunning, and persistence
To undertake this great task, let him be
Germany's leader, welding unity,
Annexing neutral States, for war lays bare
Mankind's barbaric bestiality.
Winners must wash civility in wounds
And hate the enemy with heart and soul,
Afraid of pity, not of cruelty
That's disciplined to free the Fatherland.
This is my gift to my own people; this
My battle-cry to necessary war!

Spotlight off to black.

SCENE TWENTY

LOUIS VOGEL *'s house.* LOUIS VOGEL, HENRIETTE,
and KLEIST *lying on the floor.*

VOGEL   No; Kleist's alive: unconscious, but still
                  breathing.

HENRIETTE   How has he done it?

VOGEL   Opium overdose.
          Equally important, Henriette;
          Why?

HENRIETTE   A thousand reasons. Look! His cheeks
         Like rain-swept clouds after a windy night

Colour with warmth. He sees his friends
          succeed –
Adam Müller made Privy Councillor –
But not himself. Cotta rejects one play
For publication – and won't pay what's due.
Iffland has ruled out a production at
The National Theatre because the Queen's
Brother objects a German officer
Would not show weakness when faced with his
          grave.
That's two plays wrecked.

VOGEL   He doesn't help his case.
Didn't he answer Iffland: 'What a shame
I made the lead – Käthchen – a girl! Next time
She'll be a boy, and you'll be overjoyed.'
A witty porcupine punctures good will.

HENRIETTE   That's all right when the sun beats on your face,
There's a light breeze, the meadow's being
          scythed,
And all the world seems good. The recent death
Of generous Queen Louise affected Heinrich:
His salary from her came to an end.
He's lost his patron Baron Altenstein
Because that cabinet's fallen. He's distraught,
Disgusted that Napoleon has married
(Thanks to Prince Metternich) our
          Archduchess
Of Austria – now Empress of the French!
This, with the Franco-Prussian alliance, means
Peace perhaps, but all Prussian officers
Will have to fight for, not against, the French!
He moves.

KLEIST   Thank you. In a moment I'll stand.

VOGEL   Heinrich: although I, and Pauline our daughter
Dearly love her mother, if you both
Ask me to release our Henriette

To you, please say: gently. I'll leave you two
Alone to think – but it will break our hearts.
(Exit)

SCENE TWENTY-ONE

HENRIETTE   My love! How are you feeling?

KLEIST   Like the dawn
             Half dark and half elated.

HENRIETTE   Dearest, do
             You think the time has come to say out loud
             What we have each been thinking? When you
                 swore
             (Do you still?) to do anything I asked ...

KLEIST   A Prussian officer will keep his word.

HENRIETTE   Then kill me, love. End my pain. Oh, I know
             You won't. No real men are left on earth!
             But this clawed cancer tearing at my womb
             Cannot be cured. All that's ahead is pain
             Deepening to a slow, despairing wait.
             I asked my husband. He was merely shocked.
             I can't bear Paulinchen sob while I scream.

KLEIST   That line of Hölderlin rings in my head:
             'My heart belongs already to the dead'.
             My better self, my future, and my love:
             Ten years ago, one rainy, spring March day,
             I walked with Ernst von Pfuel and Otto
                 Rühle –
             Both of whom joined our regiment as ensigns –
             To the pine woods above the smaller Wannsee.
             There, as we let the sandy soil drift through
             Our fingers, we worked out how best to end

Our lives: row to the middle of the lake,
Our pockets filled with rocks, and pull the
        trigger.
My cousin, Carl Otto von Pannwitz and I
(Yes, we shared boyhood tutors) swore in blood
We'd take our lives if necessary – and he did;
Fresh from the Polish fighting, on my birthday.
So Jettchen; you see? I am well prepared
To consummate our love by killing us.

HENRIETTE   My Heinrich, greatest love is proved in death.
Let's go back to the Wannsee, and redeem
Your word? Beside the Friedrich-Wilhelm
        bridge
There is an inn where we can stay. It's called
The New Jug. In November there'll be rooms,
And we'll be private there, choosing our time.
I'll tell my darling Vogel I am off,
Briefly to Potsdam, and ask him to call
His carriage.

KLEIST   What strange feelings we two share!
Let's pack, and write our final letters there.
Then, like two wild balloonists, far above
Our sufferings, elated, seal our love.

SCENE TWENTY-TWO

GOETHE *and* CHARLOTTE VON STEIN.

GOETHE   Thank you for seeing me. Do you keep well?

CHARLOTTE   I live.

GOETHE   I've come to ask a favour of you.
Lotte Schiller's birthday this year is
Important to her. We have as her present
A seven-drawered writing desk. Charlotte, if you

Would invite her out, any time you like,
We could install it while she is away.

CHARLOTTE   Of course. I'll send a note round.

GOETHE   I will go
With it to her, to save time, if you like.

CHARLOTTE   You can waste a lot of time, saving time.

GOETHE   All right. Perhaps you and your married niece
Amalia will come to see my coins?
May I invite you?

CHARLOTTE   Frau von Helvig may
Be free. You can invite us.

GOETHE   Oh, my Lotte!
Why don't you visit me every Thursday at
Eleven o'clock, and bring your friends; then I
Can share my works of art. We can discuss them.
Come to my Sunday concerts! Hear us read ...

CHARLOTTE   With all the overstress of the amateur.

GOETHE   I'll be away a longer time than some
Might wish, shortly.

CHARLOTTE   Going where?

GOETHE   To Karlsbad.

CHARLOTTE   Oh, to the springs where we two used to go!

GOETHE   While I'm away, please would you show just
             some
Goodwill towards my wife and son?

CHARLOTTE   Although
It is not pleasant for me to unseal

Old wounds, as you so love her, just this once
I'll ask both round to spend an evening with
me.

GOETHE   It is the quiet honours that mean much.
As my night's coming cloudbergs break at day
My son will gild my setting.

CHARLOTTE   Let him taste
A little less champagne. Seventeen glasses,
In a club of his mother's class, he drank.

GOETHE   I know, I know. Oh, Lotte, my high star –
To you and Shakespeare I owe what I am.

CHARLOTTE   A fine comparison! I am remote
As one long dead in a far distant land,
Seen high in the cold vault of darkness?

GOETHE   No!
To a new truth what is more hurtful than
Old error?

CHARLOTTE   What is past cannot return.

GOETHE   Coal is revived by incense, and so prayer
Revives the heart's hopes ...

CHARLOTTE   If a spark is there.

SCENE TWENTY-THREE

The New Jug Inn.
HENRIETTE *and* KLEIST.

HENRIETTE   These two rooms on the top floor each look out
Over the Kleiner Wannsee!
                    (*Calling off-stage*) Thank you! Frau

Stimming, could some coffee be brought out
To the green area beside the lake?

KLEIST   November days grow short. *(Calling off-stage)*
                And some rum, too?

HENRIETTE   A table and two chairs – yes, we will pay!
                (To KLEIST*)* Oh my love, have you written all you
                    want?
                My basket's covered with our fiery babes
                Inside. No one will guess. She says we smile.

KLEIST   We do! Serene, contented, I have made
                My peace with Sophie von Haza, Ulrike
                My sister, and my once-loved Marie Kleist –
                No! Still-loved! – writing in a paean of triumph
                How your soul flies like a young eagle, who
                Gives up for me your own, your dearest
                    daughter –
                Far more lovely than the morning sun,
                A father who devotes himself to you,
                 A husband so good, loving you will seek
                Your happiness in place of his. I tell
                You understand my sadness is sublime,
                Vast-rooted, beyond cure: an ecstasy
                More like an angel's – and I now can pray
                And thank God for my tortured, wretched life
                And His last gift: glorious, voluptuous death.
                Ah! I am happy! All that saddens us
                Is the deep grief that we will leave behind.
                'Know that it was our choice, and we shall meet
                Hereafter in a better world, where kings
                Do not sell armies to the enemy,
                Where there is no more pain. So, feel our joy.
                Her grave is dearer to me than the beds
                Of all the Empresses that rule the world!'

HENRIETTE   'Vogel, excellent husband, do not grieve.
                Don't weep. You know what lay ahead for me.
                You will protect our little one far more

Than I would have been able to. Give her
My kiss. And please, dear Louis, bury me
With Kleist, faithful companion in my death
As in life. By the Wannsee let us rest.'

SCENE TWENTY-FOUR

WIELAND *and* GOETHE.

WIELAND

Are Kleist and Henriette Vogel dead?
By the Wannsee?

GOETHE

                They walked down to the shore
And crossed the bridge to take the Summer Path.
Old Riebisch rested on his wheelbarrow,
Blocking the way. Kleist smiled and asked him
      to
Help this lady pass; tipped him a groschen,
To his delight. The old man met his wife
Bringing up cups and saucers, scolding away
That these two want to have their coffee out
In creeping mist as cold November wanes.
'They'll make it worth your while!' he grinned.
      'This will
Be cold before it's there!' she shouted back.
She knew the guests were merry, but they
      played
Like children, chasing, running down the hill
Laughing and larking as the sunlight failed.
They threw flat stones to skim the idle lake
Merging to densening air-held water-drops.
Frau Riebisch reached them. Her husband had
      brought
The chairs and table. She served them. They
      laughed
And threw good money in a cup; thanked her
And sent her muttering on her way: 'It's odd.

That woman's tied black ribbon round her
    ankles.
She has a basket pressing down the heather
Covered with a white napkin. It was heavy.'
Pine trees looked dark now. The damp air was
    chill,
And fog thickened what little light remained.
Frau Riebisch found the path below,then heard
A shot. 'What are they playing at?' she puffed;
'Where did they find a gun?' At Wilhelm
    Bridge
She heard another shot, startling late birds.
Then, as the echo faded, it was night.

WIELAND   There is an end to tears. My son Ludwig
Would hear him read his works aloud, cheer on,
Encourage Kleist. He saw in him our future,
And brought him home. I was near seventy;
He twenty-five. My youngest daughter loved
    him;
And Kleist read part of his *Death of Guiscard*
To me. What I heard was quite beyond praise.

GOETHE   Everything's over. Just one thing remains.
Nature has lent us tears, the cry of pain,
When we can bear no more. What suffering
Must have gnawed him to leave his talent,
    which
In his tormented life was talisman
Of happiness! Yes, I was fond of him,
And tried to help, but deep morbidity
Destroyed him as a writer and a man.

WIELAND   We must mourn, and move on. These war-
    drenched days
Sweep all aside. Deserted Moscow burns:
A jewel of centuries, the size of Paris –
Five hundred palaces besides the Tsar's –
That superb city, in a single week
Reduced to icy desert's windy ash.

> If men like you despair, withdraw, to leave
> Politics to the men of iron and blood
> Who will restrain? Who teach men how to
>   grieve?
> The Marseillaise and guillotine's red flood
> Will wash all Europe, and the years to come
> Know only slaughter, and the fife and drum.

GOETHE   Enough! The stage grows dark. Look!
(To audience)

> Over each hill
>   Is quiet.
> Tree-tops still
>   Their riot
> To scarcely a breath.
> Leafy birds sleep;
> Wait. Do not weep.
> Soon you will rest.

Fade to black. As the applause dies down,
Tchaikovsky's '1812', from bar 307 to end.

FINIS.

A Religion of Culture

Review by Arnd Kerkhecker,
Fellow and Tutor in Classics,
Worcester College, Oxford.

OXFORD MAGAZINE, March 1997

A play, not just about Goethe, but about *Goethe's Weimar* (thirty-three characters, among them Goethe, Schiller, Wieland, Herder, Hölderlin, Kleist, the Duchess—not the Duke—, Napoleon, Talleyrand, Metternich . . .); set in Weimar, Jena, Erfurt, Frankfurt, Berlin . . .; extending over almost twenty years (1794–1812)—what would Goethe have said? *Shakespeare und kein Ende*, perhaps. Perhaps even 'ingenious thoroughness / Does not make up for a swift-moving plot' (as he says to Kleist in this play). But that would be Goethe in one of his more carping and opinionated moods, in one of his (rarer) moments of Aristotelian orthodoxy. The English playwright exercising his dramatic birthright can easily defend this rich mosaic of vignettes by appealing to Goethe's own infatuation with Shakespeare (in Wieland's translation, of course—Goethe to Wieland: 'But I prefer—even though some is changed— / Your own.'). This is a study in '*Weimar* as a mode of spiritual life', as Thomas Mann might have called it: the spirit of the place reflected in a swift series of sparkling encounters, bewildering in its variety, stirring in its epic scope.

The vision was conveyed through some splendid acting. Goethe's (Daniel Cassiel) youthfulness did not diminish his *gravitas*. Schiller (Ian Drysdale), though craving the older man's attention, yet came across as the fermenting, perhaps leading, intellect in their friendship (in their first conversation after Batsch's lecture in Jena on 20 July 1794). Hölderlin (William Greener) was refreshingly vigorous (more satyr than seraph), and this made his first ill-fated encounter with Goethe look revealingly different from his own account (in a letter to Neuffer of November 1794).

The female cast was particularly impressive. The Duchess (Flavia Kenyon) appeared as a figure of arresting dignity and, amid all the entertainments and distractions of her court, of quiet loneliness; she amply deserves the fine tribute paid her after her death. Then there is Charlotte von Stein (Alice Hart Dyke), scorned (or so she believes) and suitably furious; Lotte von Schiller (Emily Dickos), ebullient and engaging; the calm and radiant simplicity of Goethe's Christiane (Kathy Tozer), unsullied by malevolent insinuation; Susette Gontard's (Josephine Higgs) teasing allure; the profound darkness of Henriette Vogel's (Gayle Ashley) narcotic morbidity: all conjured up with perfect ease and conviction.

Among the minor parts, the sprightly lady-in-waiting Thusnelda (Chaon Cross) deserves to be mentioned. So does the standard-bearer (Philip Meyer). At the audience with Napoleon, his sustained (silent) hauteur culminated in a splendidly dismissive wave of the hand sending *Monsieur Goet* on his way after the *Empereur* had finished with him. Nor shall we forget Luise Wieland (Miranda Warner), or Lord von Haza's little boy (Benedict Warner).

The costumes, too, were a pleasure to behold: evocative of the restrained taste of the time, and in sharp and effective contrast with the sombre splendour of the setting in the Cathedral. This was a thought-provoking juxtaposition—what is one to make of it?

From the very first scene—the memorial service for Lenz held in Weimar in the Lutheran Town Church of St Peter and St Paul—the flow of great names never ebbs. Here they are, the secular saints of German *Kulturreligion*. The play turns into a German mystery play—but a mystery play without salvation. The opening recalls the death of Lenz, and by the end, Hölderlin has absconded into madness, and the Duchess, Schiller, Herder, Kleist are all dead, most of their hopes and ambitions unfulfilled. In the case of Kleist longing to fight the French, this casts a gloomy chill on what one might hope for the future:

> If any man has courage,
> Fanaticism, cunning, and persistence
> To undertake this great task, let him be

Germany's leader, welding unity,
Annexing neutral States, for war lays bare
Mankind's barbaric bestiality.

No hope for salvation here. (Wieland to Goethe: 'He is a genius; yet he's odd at meals.')

However, this is not all there is. This play is not about abstract ideas—Goethe's famous retort to Schiller suits its new home perfectly:

Schiller, I'm very pleased to find I have
Ideas without my knowing it.

This play is about people, some more, some less noble, but all noble in their efforts and, in Faustian fashion, 'ever striving'. Ideas (only?) matter, because they have had them. This is how Herder talks to Hölderlin about Hegel: 'You, / I hear, in student days in Tübingen, / Shared a room with that thorough Jacobin / Hegel?'

In the end, what counts is language, the language of poetry (as Herder would have been the first to insist). The verse is effortless and pure, and rises on occasion to noble resonance. Goethe to Kleist:

The world, / Dear Kleist, is a cracked bell at best.

Müller to Haza:

You might as well attempt to hide the wind
As lock appreciation in your heart.

. . . —I shall not even begin to excerpt Hölderlin's part—his strained, clear tone is beautifully caught. (Less convincing, perhaps, the bold zeugma in Goethe's line to Charlotte von Stein: 'Look at the moon! Our river! Both are full.')

For readers of German literature, this language holds special delights. In addition to the poems and the plays, the novels and the essays, contemporary letters, diaries, reported conversations are continually present. Much learning, lightly worn, has gone into this play. The poet's quotations, 'dug up, transplanted with their roots . . . into his garden', have come into full and fragrant blossom.

An example. At the end of the play, the audience is left with a masterly translation of the most celebrated of Goethe's, perhaps of all German poems (*Über allen Gipfeln / ist Ruh*):

> Over each hill
> Is quiet.
> Tree-tops still
> Their riot
> To scarcely a breath.
> Leafy birds sleep;
> Wait. Do not weep.
> Soon you will rest.

The end is sombre, indeed. This mystery play promises no salvation. The way into the dark is suggestively signposted throughout the play by the use of music. The action begins to the sounds of the *Alleluia* of 'So recent-lost, young Wolfgang Mozart'. At the end of Act I, we hear Mozart's *Requiem*: Schiller dies in the eighth bar of the *Lacrimosa* (the point at which Mozart's manuscript breaks off, and we are left with Süssmayr). At the end of the play, when the stage has faded into darkness visible, there is also darkness audible: the stump-grinding exertions of Tchaikovsky's *Overture 1812*. Democritus Junior, witnessing the proceedings from his neighbouring tomb, may have discovered a new shade of grey for his melancholic palette.

The sound of cannons is a moving and fitting end to *Goethe's Weimar*. Dark prospects ahead invite the eye to glance side-wards, from Goethe's Weimar to Wieland's Ossmannstedt. Kleist to Goethe:

> Goethe, it was
> The proudest moment in my life when he
> Beside his glowing fire at Ossmannstedt
> Listened as I read out *Guiscard the Norman*.

At the end of the play, Wieland has but a year to live. He dies in Weimar, on Wednesday, 20 January, 1813, and is buried in Ossmannstedt near the bank of the river Ilm on Monday the 25th. Years later, Goethe mocked the modest iron fence enclosing Wieland's tomb. He could already see the soldiers coming to tear it apart and turn it into horseshoes (to Eckermann, 5 July 1827). Wieland's grave has so far escaped the sound of cannons and the hand of war. Goethe's coffin, laid to rest in the vault of the Dukes, has not.